# Mankind

An anonymous morality play of the fifteenth century

Edited for the Groundling Press,
and with an introduction by
Christopher Hapka

# Table of Contents

# About the Groundling Press

The Groundling Press publishes useful, readable, affordable e-book and on-demand editions of English-language plays from the sixteenth, seventeenth, and early eighteenth centuries for general readers and practical performers. Each play has been newly and carefully edited from one or more early printed texts or manuscripts. These editions are not based on any existing public-domain text.

The plays have been newly modernized from the original old-spelling texts, with the intention of creating a text that is readable and accessible to a modern reader. Spelling has been updated to conform to modern usage; however, archaic forms have been retained where they affect pronunciation or meter. Punctuation has likewise been silently modernized. Notes are provided for words and references that may be unfamiliar to the modern reader, and appendices provide interesting materials related to the text, where available.

To keep the plays affordable, they are currently available only in e-book and print-on-demand editions. Performance rights to this modernized edition are available at no charge or at a nominal fee, but permission must be sought in advance. Please visit our web site, www.groundlingpress.com, for more information.

# About Mankind

*Theater Before the Theatre*

In 1576, Richard Burbage built a playhouse in Shoreditch, then outside the jurisdiction of the City of London. The house, called simply "The Theatre," was a success, and by 1600 at least seven more had been built in and around the capital.

The construction of permanent playhouses led to an explosion of English plays written to fill them. But before these permanent stages were built, there was already theater in England. Bands of traveling players put on plays wherever a temporary stage could be constructed; most often, outdoors in an inn-yard, with the audience watching either from the ground or from the galleries of the inn.

*Mankind* is an inn-yard play, written for just this sort of performance. The characters enter through the crowd around the stage, and partway through the play a collection is taken from the audience, with the threat that if enough money is not raised, the devil, in his elaborate costume, will not appear. The script includes local in-jokes, names of prominent citizens supposed to have been visited by the play's vices. The appendix to this edition includes a more detailed discussion of how the inn-yard shaped this play, excerpted from Joseph Quincy Adams' *Shakespearean Playhouses*.

*Mankind* is a morality play, a highly formalized drama in which the personification of humanity is visited by personified virtues and vices, which battle for his soul. But *Mankind* is not a sermon; it is entertainment, and its writers and players depended on a happy audience for their livelihood.

So the play focuses on what it knows its audience wants to see. In the play, virtue is championed by Mercy, a sententious guardian angel who speaks in overcomplicated and pretentious clerical cod-Latin. For this, he is mercilessly taunted by three minor vices and their masters, Mischief and the demon Titivillus. Most of the play is given up not to Mercy's sermons, but to the banter and slapstick among the vices, as they attempt to lead Mankind to his ruin. The inn-yard allows the players to be profane, irreverent, and funny in a way that would not be possible a few decades later in a licensed playhouse.

The best English plays of the pre-Theatre period used the framework of the morality play to create works of real theatrical merit, and among those, *Mankind* stands out, not just as a document of a lost era of English theater, but as an entertaining play in its own right.

## *About the Text*

The play exists in a single manuscript, usually called the "Macro Manuscript" after Cox Macro, an eighteenth-century Church of England clergyman who owned it for a time. The Macro Manuscript, now in the archives of the Folger Shakespeare Library in Washington, D.C., also contains two other medieval morality plays: *Wisdom* and *The Castle of Perseverance.*

This edition is based on a facsimile of the original manuscript, and on the two earliest printed editions of *Mankind,* both old-spelling editions, which were printed in 1897 and 1904. The 1897 printing was part of a larger collection of pre-Shakespearean English theater; the editor, John Matthews Manly, worked from a transcription made around 1882 by Eleanor Marx, the English actress and translator (and daughter of Karl Marx). A few years later, in 1904, F.A. Furnivall and Alfred W. Pollard edited the three Macro plays in a single volume, working from both the Marx transcription and the original manuscript.

*Mankind* was written in early modern English, but it is an older English than Shakespeare's. Because of this, somewhat more editing was necessary than with a seventeenth-century text to make the language comprehensible to a modern reader. Minor grammatical changes have been made where this could be done without affecting the scan of the verse. For example, in Scene 1, Mercy says:

I haue be the very mene for yowr restytucyon

This has been rendered in the current text as:

I have been the very means for your restitution

with "be" silently modernized to "been" and "mean" to "means." Where such a change would affect the scan, a note with the modern reading is offered instead.

The Macro Manuscript does not divide *Mankind* into acts or scenes. Manly followed this in presenting the play unbroken, in its entirety. Furnivall and Pollard broke it into three scenes and an epilogue. In the current edition, the play is presented in French scenes, meaning that the scenes are defined by the entrances and exits of the characters.

The first page of the manuscript, labeled "122" by Macro or another modern owner, contains, on the front, the introductory speech by Mercy, here labeled as Scene 1, and on the back, the beginning of a scene between Mercy and Mischief, labeled here as Scene 2. At the end of this page, the manuscript indicates that the next line will belong to Mercy. But the following leaf, labeled "123," begins with a speaker, who cannot be Mercy, exhorting the band to play a dancing tune and to flog someone. The scene continues with Mischief's three assistants, Nowadays, New Guise, and Nought, taunting Mercy with their dance, with Mischief nowhere to be seen.

Clearly, part of the play is missing here; most likely a full leaf, front and back, about seventy lines. During this gap, Mischief departs and the three vices arrive. To aid performance, this edition includes a brief modern transition, written by myself, to bridge this gap between scenes one and two; it is indicated by brackets at the beginning and end of the passage.

## Sources

The following editions and secondary works provided valuable guidance and insight, as well as illuminating some obscure points. Where a specific work was relied on for a line reading or gloss, it is mentioned in the accompanying note.

- John Matthews Manly, ed., *Specimens of the Pre-Shaksperean Drama,* Vol. I. The Athenaeum Press, Boston and London, 1900.

- F.J. Furnivall and Alfred W. Pollard, ed., *The Macro Plays.* The Early English Text Society, London, 1904.

- John S. Farmer, *Recently Recovered "Lost" Tudor Plays, With Some Others.* The Early English Drama Society, London, 1909.

- W.K. Smart, "Some Notes on Mankind," in *Modern Philology,* volume 14, nos. 1, 5 (1916).

- Glynne Wickham, ed., *English Moral Interludes.* London: Dent 1976.

- Margaret Schlauch, "The Social Background of Shakespeare's Malapropisms," in *A Reader in the Language of Shakespearean Drama,* John Benjamins Publishing Company, 1987.

- Douglas Bruster and Eric Rasmussen, *Everyman and Mankind.* Arden Early English Drama, 2009.

- Christina M. Fitzgerald and John T. Sebastian, general editors, *The Broadview Anthology of Medieval Drama.* Broadview Press, 2012.

# Dramatis Personae

Mercy

Mischief

Nought

New Guise

Nowadays

Mankind

Titivillus

# MANKIND

## Scene 1

*Enter* MERCY.

*Mercy.*  The very founder and beginner of our first creation,
Among us sinful wretches he oweth to be magnified,
That for our disobedience He had no indignation*
To send His own son to be torn and crucified.
Our obsequious service to Him should be applied
Where He was lord of all and made all things of nought,
For the sinful sinner to let him* revived
And for his redemption set His own son at nought.

That may be said and verified: mankind was dear* bought.
By the piteous death of Jesu he had his remedy;
He was purged of his default, that wretchedly had wrought,
By his glorious passion, that blessed lavatory.*
O sovereigns, I beseech you your conditions to rectify
And with humility and reverence to have a remotion*

---

**He had no indignation:** In the original, "none indignation." God was not so angered by man's disobedience that He would not send His son to be crucified, as described in the next line.

**let him:** In the MS this is "lete hym." Manly (1897) suggests "late"; Furnivall and Pollard (1904) "hade." The meaning seems to be that God caused His son to be revived, or brought back to life.

**dear:** dearly.

**lavatory:** Lavatory meant either a cleansing (as here) or a place for washing; neither modern toilets nor the use of "lavatory" as a euphemism existed at the time *Mankind* was written.

**remotion:** The usual sense is "removal" or "departure"; here it seems to be more of a "going back to."

1

To this blessed Prince that our nature doth glorify,
That ye may be participable of his retribution.*

I have been the very means for your restitution;
Mercy is my name, that mourneth for your offence.
Divert not yourself in time of temptation,
That ye may be acceptable to God at your going hence.
The great mercy of God, that is of most preeminence,
By mediation* of our Lady, that is ever abundant
To the sinful creature that will repent his negligence:
I pray God, at your most need,* that Mercy be your defendant.*

In good works, I advise you, sovereigns, to be perseverant,
To purify your souls, that they be not corrupt;
For your ghostly enemy will make his avaunt*
Your good conditions if he may interrupt.
O ye sovereigns that sit, and ye brethren that stand right up,*
Prick* not your felicities in things transitory!
Behold not the earth, but lift your eye up!
See how the head the members daily do magnify.

Who is the head? Forsooth, I shall you certify:
I mean our Saviour, that was likened to a lamb.

---

**participable of his retribution:** "Participable" means to be able to
  participate; retribution did not yet have the negative sense it has in
  modern usage, but refers to a reward.

**mediation:** Intervention. The MS has "medytacyon."

**at your most need:** In your time of greatest need.

**defendant:** Defender.

**avaunt:** Advance.

**sovereigns that sit...brethren that stand:** The play would most likely have
  been performed in an inn-yard, where most of the audience would have
  stood around the stage, with the wealthier or higher-class patrons seated
  in galleries.

**prick:** May mean "to measure" or "to store." Either way, the message is that
  your happiness should not depend on transitory things.

And his saints be the members that daily he doth satisfy
With the precious river that runneth from his womb.*
There is no such food, by water nor by land,
So precious, so glorious, so redeful* to our intent.
For it hath dissolved mankind from the bitter bond
Of the mortal enemy, that venomous serpent,

From the which God preserve you all at the last judgment,
For securely there shall be a strict* examination.
The corn shall be saved, the chaff shall be brent:*
I beseech you heartily, have this premeditation.*

---

**womb:** Stomach. The reference is to the wound in Jesus' side.

**redeful:** Helpful. Some editions, including Furnivall and Pollard (1904), have "needful."

**strict:** The MS has "sterat" or "strerat," the meaning of which is unclear. If not "strict" or "straight," it may be "stern."

**brent:** Burned.

**have this premeditation:** Plan for this in advance.

# Scene 2

*Enter* MISCHIEF.

| | |
|---|---|
| *Mischief.* | I beseech you heartily, leave your calcation!* |
| | Leave your "chaff," leave your "corn," leave your dilatation!* |
| | Your wit is little, your head is mickle,* ye are full of |
| | predication.* |
| | But, sir, I pray this question* to clarify: |
| | Driff-draff, mish-mash, |
| | Some was corn, and some was chaff, |
| | My dame said my name was Raffe— |
| | Unshut your lock, and take a ha'penny! |
| | |
| *Mercy.* | Why come ye hither, brother? Ye were not desired. |
| | |
| *Mischief.* | For* a winter corn-thresher, sir, I have hired; |
| | And ye said the corn should be saved and the chaff should be |
| | fired, |
| | And he proveth nay, as it showeth by this verse: |
| | *"Corn servit bredibus, chaff servit horsibus, straw firebusque."** |

---

**calcation:** An archaic term for treading out juice from grapes. Mischief is using this Latinate form to mock Mercy's own high-flown language.

**dilatation:** Another Latinate term for spreading or expanding, referring to Mercy's sermon that opened the play.

**mickle:** Large or great.

**predication:** Preaching or sermonizing.

**question:** Subject or problem; Mischief is pretending to give Mercy a new text to expound upon.

**for:** Because.

***Corn servit bredibus...:*** Mischief mocks Mercy again in false Latin, pointing out that the pious sermon does not match actual farming practice. The sense, as Mischief goes on to explain, is "Corn is used for bread; chaff is used for horses; straw is burnt for warmth."

This is as much to say, to your lewd* understanding,
As, the corn shall serve to bread at the next baking;
*"Chaff horsibus, et reliquid,"**
The chaff, to horse shall be good produce;
When a man is for-cold,* the straw may be brent,
And so forth, et cetera.

Mercy.      Avoid,* good brother! Ye be culpable
            To interrupt thus my talking delectable.

Mischief.   Sir, I have neither horse nor saddle,
            Therefore I may not ride.

Mercy.      Hie you forth on foot, brother, in God's name!

Mischief.   I say, sir, I am come hither to make you game;*
            Yet bade ye me not go out in the Devil's name,
            And I will abide.*

[Mercy.*    Brother Mischief, stay not here to harass Mankind

---

**lewd:** Base or uneducated.

*et reliquid*: And the rest; and so on.

**for-cold:** Very cold. The "for" is a middle English prefix meaning "completely" or "excessively."

**avoid:** Go away.

**make you game:** Make fun of you; taunt you.

**abide:** Stay.

**[Mercy...:** As explained in the introduction, a leaf appears to be missing here in the manuscript, during which Mischief would have exited and the three vices would have entered. In this edition, the current editor has provided a brief original transition (the last two speeches of this scene and the first line of the next) that may be used in performance; the actual missing section is certainly much longer, about as long as Scene 1 and the surviving portion of Scene 2.

With devilish wit, new guise and new thought,
Mankind should not by new guise be made blind,
For your new guise of nowadays shall come to naught.

*Mischief.*    Brother Mercy, as you say, so shall it be:
I shall depart myself, but my three followers,
Nowadays, New Guise, and Nought, shall follow me,
And turn Mankind to our party from yours.

# Scene 3

*Exit* MISCHIEF. *Enter* NOUGHT, NEW GUISE, *and*
NOWADAYS.

*New Guise.* Come, brothers, let us dance,]
And ho, minstrels, play the common trace.ᐩ
Lay on with the baleisᐩ till his belly burst!

*Nought.* I put caseᐩ I break my neck; how then?

*New Guise.* I give no force,ᐩ by Saint Anne!ᐩ

*Nowadays.* Leap about lively! Thou art a wightᐩ man;
Let us be merry while we be here!

*Nought.* Shall I break my neck to show you sport?

*Nowadays.* Therefore ever beware of thy report.

*Nought.* I beshrewᐩ ye all! Here is a shrewdᐩ sort;
Have thereᐩ at them, with a merry cheer!

---

**trace:** Dance.

**baleis:** A rod or switch for flogging.

**I put case:** Supposing.

**I give no force:** I don't care.

**Saint Anne:** In Christian tradition, mother of the Virgin Mary. This oath
survives today in the form "Mother of Mary." The MS has "Sent Tanne."

**wight:** Strong, brave.

**beshrew:** Curse.

**shrewd:** Ill-tempered, accursed.

**there:** The intended reading is unclear, but may be "therefore."

*Here they dance.**

| | |
|---|---|
| *Mercy.* | Do way!* Do way this revel, sirs, do way! |
| *Nowadays.* | "Do way," good Adam,* "do way!"<br>This is no part of thy play. |
| *Nought.* | Yes, marry, I pray you! For I love not this reveling.<br>Come* forth, good father, I you pray;<br>By a little ye may assay.<br>Anon off with your clothes if ye will pray.<br>Go to, for I have had a pretty scuttling. |
| *Mercy.* | Nay, brother, I will not dance. |
| *New Guise.* | If ye will, sir, my brother will make you to prance. |
| *Nowadays.* | With all my heart, sir, if I may you advance.*<br>Ye may assay* by a little trace.* |

---

**Here they dance:** This is one of the few stage directions in the manuscript. On the side of the page, where ordinarily it would identify the next speaker, it says: "Here they dance. Mercy sayeth:"

**Do way:** Stop, put aside. Cf. Chaucer's Second Nun's Tale ("Do way thy ignorance...and sacrifice to our goddess.")

**Adam:** Generic address for a man, in this case presumably Mercy.

**Come:** Unclear in MS. Some editions have "even".

**advance:** Improve, teach.

**assay:** Make an attempt.

**trace:** A step often used at the beginning of medieval dances.

| | |
|---|---|
| *Nought.* | Ye, sir, will ye do well? |
| | Trace not with them, be my counsel. |
| | I tell,* it is a narrow space. |
| | But, sir, I trow, of us three I heard you speak.* |
| *New Guise.* | Christ's curse had ye, therefore, for I was asleep. |
| *Nowadays.* | And I had the cup in my hand, ready to go to meat.* |
| | Therefore, sir, curtly* grett you well.* |
| *Mercy.* | Few words; few and well set!* |
| *New Guise.* | Sir, it is the new guise and the new jet:* |
| | Many words and shortly set. |
| | This is the new guise, every deal.* |
| *Mercy.* | Lady, help! How wretches delight in their sinful ways! |
| *Nowadays.* | Say nought against the new guise nowadays. |
| | Thou shall find us shrewish at all assays.* |
| | Beware! You may soon lick a buffet.* |

---

**I tell:** I tell you.

**of us three I heard you speak:** Presumably, on the missing leaf between scenes 2 and 3, Mercy made a speech invoking "Nought," "New Guise" (i.e., fashion), and "Nowadays."

**go to meat:** Eat a meal.

**curtly:** Briefly; quickly.

**grett you well:** The meaning is unclear; either Nowadays is saying that they are greeting Mercy rudely because they have been interrupted by him naming them in his (lost) speech, or he is asking Mercy to speak quickly.

**set:** Placed.

**guise...jet:** Fashion; custom.

**every deal:** Everywhere; in every place.

**shrewish at all assays:** Spiteful or vicious at each attempt.

**lick a buffet:** Taste a blow.

| | |
|---|---|
| *Mercy.* | He was well occupied that brought you,* brethren. |
| *Nought.* | I heard you call "New Guise," "Nowadays," "Nought:" all these three together.<br>If ye say that I lie, I shall make you to slither!*<br>So take you here a tripet!* |
| *Mercy.* | Say me your names; I know you not. |
| *New Guise.* | New Guise I! |
| *Nowadays.** | I, Nowadays. |
| *Nought.** | I, Nought. |
| *Mercy.* | By Jesu Christ, that me dear bought,<br>Ye betray many men.* |
| *New Guise.* | Betray? Nay, nay, sir; nay, nay.<br>We make them both fresh and gay.*<br>But of your name, sir, I you pray,<br>That we may you ken!* |

---

**brought you:** Summoned you here.

**slither:** Crawl or creep.

**tripet:** Trip; presumably Nought trips Mercy at this point in the action.

***Nowadays...Nought:*** In the manuscript, all three names are written on one line, indicated as spoken by New Guise. The "I" before or after each name is also unclear. It is possible the author intended New Guise to introduce all three characters; however, modern editors generally allow the other two to introduce themselves.

**many men:** The manuscript is unclear here; it appears "many a man" has been crossed out and "many men" written in its place.

**fresh and gay:** Youthful; cheerful; lively; lusty.

**ken:** Know.

| | |
|---|---|
| *Mercy.* | Mercy is my name and my denomination.<sup></sup> |
| | I conceive ye have but a little force<sup></sup> in my communication. |
| *New Guise.* | Ei, ei!<sup></sup> Your body is full of English Latin. |
| | To have this English made in Latin<sup></sup> |
| | I am afeared it will brest<sup></sup> |
| *Nowadays.* | I pray you heartily, worshipful clerk, |
| | "Pravote!" quoth the butcher unto me<sup></sup> |
| | When I stole a leg full of mutton: |
| | "I have eaten a dish full of curds, |
| | And I have shitten your mouth full of turds." |
| | You are a strong, cunning clerk,<sup></sup> I pray, |
| | Now open your satchel of Latin words |
| | And say me this in clerical manner. |

---

**denomination:** An intentionally pretentious word for name or title.

**force:** This word is unclear in the manuscript; if "fors," it could signify confidence or weight. Manly (1897) gives "fors;" Furnivall (1904) gives "faus."

**Ei, ei:** A Middle English interjection indicating surprise or anger.

**To have this English made in Latin...:** From this point up until Nowadays' "Ye are a strong, cunning clerk, I pray," several lines are written in the margin, and their place in the text, or if they have a place in this text, is unclear. Both Manly (1897) and Furnivall (1904) render these lines as a single marginal note; however, they seem more likely to be insertions by the copyist. For this edition, they have been inserted into the text in what appear to be the appropriate places.

**brest:** Burst.

**"Pravote!" quoth the butcher unto me:** This marginal line is more or less illegible in the MS. Manly (1897) gives it as "I rausch, quod the naeger on-to me;" Furnivall (1904) gives "It ram be quod the bocher on-to me." This edition adopts the reading of Wickham (1976), among others, with "Pravote!" meaning "I curse you." While having the advantage of sense, this reading is difficult to find in the manuscript.

**clerk:** Clergyman; cleric.

|  |  |
|---|---|
|  | Also, I have a wife; her name is Rachel; |
|  | betwixt her and me was a great battle, |
|  | And fain* of you I would hear tell |
|  | Who was the most master. |

*Nought.*  Thy wife Rachel, I dare lay twenty lice!

*Nowadays.*  Who spoke to ye, fool? Thou art not wise!
Go and do that longeth* to thine office:
*Osculare fundamentum!**

*Nought.*  Lo, master! Lo, here is a pardon* belly meat;*
It is granted of* Pope Pocket.
If ye will put your nose in his wife's socket,
Ye shall have forty days of pardon.

*Mercy.*  This idle language ye shall repent!
Out of this place I would ye went!*

---

**fain:** [I would be] eager or pleased.

**longeth:** Belonging.

***Osculare fundamentum*:** Kiss my ass.

**pardon:** A document showing that an indulgence, the formal forgiveness of sins, had been granted. The buying and selling of pardons, especially by professional pardoners, was a target for satire in the medieval period.

**belly meat:** Likely a reference to 1 Corinthians 6:13: "Meats for the belly, and the belly for meats: but God shall destroy both it and them." The same line is referenced in Chaucer's Pardoner's Tale. It also serves as a pun; "meet" means "satisfy." In both cases, the meaning is that his pardon will satisfy Nowadays' demands.

**of:** By.

**I would ye went:** I would like you to go.

*New Guise.* Go we hence all three with one assent.
My father is irk of* our eloquence;
Therefore I will no longer tarry.
God bring you, master, and blessed Mary,
To the number of the demonical friary!

*Nowadays.* Come wind, come rain,
Though I come never again.
The devil put out both your eyen!*
Fellows, go we hence tight.*

*Nought.* Go we hence, a devil way!*
Here is the door, here is the way.
Farewell, gentle Geoffrey;*
I pray God give you good night.

*Exit* NOUGHT, NEW GUISE, *and* NOWADAYS.

---

**irk of:** Irked with; annoyed by.

**eyen:** Eyes.

**tight:** Properly; perhaps quickly.

**a devil way:** A common emphatic way of saying "away".

**Farewell, gentle Geoffrey:** Apparently a common set phrase or proverb at
the time.

# Scene 4

MERCY, *alone*

Mercy.　Thanked be God, we have a fair deliverance
　　　　Of these three unthrifty* guests.
　　　　They know full* little what is their ordinance;*
　　　　I prove, by reason, they be worse than beasts:
　　　　A beast doth after his natural institution;*
　　　　Ye may conceive, by their disport* and behaviour,
　　　　Their joy and delight is in derision
　　　　Of their own Christ, to his dishonour.

　　　　This condition of living, it is prejudicial;*
　　　　Beware thereof! It is worse than any felony or treason.
　　　　How may it be excused before the Justice* of all,
　　　　When for every idle word we must* yield a reason?
　　　　They have great case;* therefore they will take no thought;

---

**unthrifty:** Unworthy, wicked.

**full:** Very.

**their ordinance:** The way in which they ought to behave.

**natural institution:** Nature; instinct.

**disport:** Carries the sense both of an entertainment or "sport" and of "deportment" or manner.

**prejudicial:** Harmful.

**Justice:** Judge; in this case, God.

**we must:** The manuscript appears to say "ws must," which the writer could have intended as either "we must" or "us must."

**case:** The meaning is unclear. It could be a continuation of the legal metaphor, referring to a law case; or it could refer to the meaning of case as luck or circumstances; in other words, since they are enjoying themselves now, they are not thinking of the consequences. Some editors have suggested "ease" as an alternate reading for "case."

But how, then, when the angel of heaven shall blow the
    trump,˚
And say to the transgressors that wickedly hath wrought,
"Come forth unto your judge, and yield your account!"

Then shall I, Mercy, begin sore to weep;
Neither comfort nor counsel there shall none be had,
But such as they have sown, such shall they reap:
They be wanton now, but then shall they be sad.˚
The good new guise˚ nowadays I will not disallow;
I discommend˚ the vicious˚ guise; I pray have me excused:˚
I need not to speak of it, your reason will tell it you;
Take that is˚ to be taken, and leave that is to be refused.

---

**trump:** Trumpet.

**sad:** Serious.

**guise:** Fashion; custom.

**discommend:** Advise against. Mercy is saying that he does not condemn all
    new fashions; only those that are bad in themselves.

**vicious:** Sinful; unwholesome; immoral.

**have me excused:** Excuse me; hold me excused.

**that is:** That which is [suitable].

# Scene 5

*Enter* MANKIND.

*Mankind.*    Of the earth and of the clay we have our propagation;
By the providence of God, thus be we derived,
To whose mercy I recommend this whole congregation:
I hope, unto his bliss, ye be all predestinate,
Every man for his degree, I trust, shall be participate.*
If we will mortify our carnal condition,
And our voluntary desires, that ever be perversionate,*
To renounce these, and yield us under God's provision.*

My name is Mankind: I have my composition*
Of a body and of a soul, of condition contrary;
Betwixt the twain is a great division.
He that should be a subject, now he hath the victory;
This is, to me, a lamentable story,
To see my flesh of my soul have governance.
Where the goodwife* is master, the goodman* may be sorry;
I may* both sigh* and sob, this is a piteous remembrance.

---

**for his degree...shall be participate:** Shall share according to his deserts.

**perversionate:** Wicked; perverted; corrupted. Does not carry the exclusively sexual connotation of the modern term.

**provision:** Providence; protecting care.

**have my composition:** Am composed.

**goodwife...goodman:** Wife...husband.

**I may...:** This line and the next appear in the margin of the manuscript, and their exact position in the text, if any, is uncertain. The second line is unclear; some editors have suggested "And in my soul," "O in my soul," or "O thou my soul."

**sigh:** "Syth" in the original manuscript; the intended pronunciation is unclear.

O thou my soul, so subtle in thy substance,
Alas! What was thy fortune and thy chance
To be associate with my flesh, that stinking dung-hill?
Lady, help! Sovereigns, it doth my soul much ill
To see the flesh prosperous and the soul trodden under foot.
I shall go to yonder man, and assay* him I will;
I trust of ghostly* solace he will be my boot.*

All hail, seemly* father! Ye be welcome to this house.
Of the very* wisdom ye have participation.*
My body with my soul is ever querulous;*
I pray you, for Saint Charity,* of your supportation.*
I beseech you heartily of your ghostly comfort.*
I am unsteadfast* in living; my name is Mankind.
My ghostly* enemy, the devil, will have a great disport*
In simple guiding if he may see me end.*

---

**assay:** Test; investigate.

**ghostly:** Spiritual.

**boot:** Advantage; relief; healing; salvation; redemption.

**seemly:** Of pleasant appearance.

**very:** True.

**participation:** A share.

**querulous:** Argumentative or litigious.

**for Saint Charity:** The original is "for sent charyte". There is a Saint Charity in the Catholic calendar, an apocryphal second-century Christian martyred under Hadrian along with her sisters Faith and Hope and her mother Sophia.

**supportation:** Assistance; moral support.

**of your ghostly comfort:** For spiritual solace from you.

**unsteadfast:** Unsteady, not firm in purpose.

**ghostly:** Spiritual.

**disport:** Amusement; a pleasant pastime.

**In simple guiding if he may see me end:** There is no wholly satisfying reading for this line. As it stands, it may mean "If he can destroy me easily." Some editors have suggested the second word should be "sinful," with a meaning of "If he can destroy me with his sinful guidance."

| | |
|---|---|
| *Mercy.* | Christ send you good comfort! Ye be welcome, my friend. |
| | Stand up on your feet; I pray you arise. |
| | My name is Mercy; ye be to me full hend.* |
| | To eschew vice I will you advise. |
| | |
| *Mankind.* | O Mercy! Of all grace and virtue ye are the well!* |
| | I have heard tell of* right worshipful* clerks,* |
| | Ye be approximate* to God, and near of his counsel,* |
| | He hath institute* you above all his works. |
| | Oh! Your lovely works to my soul are sweeter than honey! |
| | |
| *Mercy.* | The temptation of the flesh ye must resist like a man, |
| | For there is ever a battle betwixt the soul and the body: |
| | *Vita hominis est militia super terram.** |
| | Oppress* your ghostly* enemy, and be Christ's own knight; |
| | Be never a coward against your adversary. |
| | If ye will be crowned,* ye must needs fight; |
| | Intend well, and God will be your auditory.* |

---

**full hend:** Very welcome; literally, "entirely well-bred."

**well:** Source.

**of:** From.

**worshipful:** Holy.

**clerks:** Clergymen.

**approximate:** Close.

**near of his counsel:** A close advisor.

**institute:** Established; ordained.

***Vita hominis est militia super terram:*** An approximate quotation from the Old Testament, Job 7:1; "Is not a man's life upon earth a battle?"

**Oppress:** Overcome; crush.

**ghostly:** Spiritual.

**crowned:** Rewarded; admitted to heaven.

**auditory:** Audience; congregation.

Remember, my friend, the time of continuance;˙
So help me, God, it is but a cherry time.˙
Spend it well; serve God with heart's affiance;˙
Distemper˙ not your brain with good ale nor with wine.
Measure˙ is treasure: I forbid you not the use.
Measure yourself ever; beware of excess.
The superfluous guise˙ I will that you refuse;
When nature is sufficed, anon˙ that ye cease!
If a man have a horse, and keep him not too high,˙
He may then rule him at his own desire.
If he be fed overwell, he will disobey,
And, in hap,˙ cast his master in the mire.˙

*New Guise (offstage).*˙

Ye say true, sir; ye are no faitour.˙
I have fed my wife so well, till she is my master,

---

**the time of continuance:** The time your life lasts.

**cherry time:** A fleeting time, like the time of the cherry harvest.

**affiance:** Confident reliance; trust; faith.

**Distemper:** Upset; make ill.

**Measure**: Moderation; proper proportion.

**guise:** Fashion; custom.

**anon:** Immediately.

**keep him not too high:** Does not overfeed him.

**in hap:** Perhaps.

**mire:** Mud.

***New Guise (offstage):*** The text does not specify that New Guise, Nowadays, and Nought speak from offstage in this scene, but it is implied in the following dialogue. In an inn-yard performance, they may have delivered their lines from a gallery, or from the audience.

**faitour:** Faker; impostor; deceiver.

I have a great wound on my head; lo, and thereon layeth a
plaster,*
And another there* I pyse my peson.*
An* my wife were your horse, she would you all to-sanne;*
Ye feed your horse in measure;* ye are a wise man.
I trow,* an* ye were the king's palfreyman,*
A good horse should be gesum.*

Mankind.    Where speaks this fellow? Will he not come near?

Mercy.    All too soon, I fear me, my brother, for you.
He was here right now,* by Him who bought me dear,

---

**plaster:** Bandage.

**there:** Where.

**pyse my peson:** Literally, to poise (balance) a certain type of scale, though the
meaning here is the male genitals. "Pyse" is a pun on the word "piss" and
"peson" may have been a slang term for a penis and testicles, as medieval
scales of this type were said to consist of a long scale and two weights.

**An:** If.

**all to-sanne:** Argue or disagree vehemently; likely also be a pun on "samne," a
word used to describe a mating animal. The word "sanne" is unclear in
the manuscript, and later editors disagree on the reading, with some
suggesting "sane," "samne," or even "ban," to curse.

**in measure:** Moderately; prudently.

**I trow:** I trust; I believe.

**an:** if.

**palfreyman:** One who takes care of horses; a groom.

**gesum:** The meaning is unclear. Some editors, including Manly (1900) suggest
"geson," scarce; however, Furnivall (1904) suggests the opposite
meaning, "gersuma," plentiful.

**right now:** Very recently; just now.

With other of his fellows; they ken⁺ much sorrow.
They will be here right soon, if I ought⁺ depart.
Think on my doctrine;⁺ it shall be your defense.
Learn while I am here; set my words in heart,⁺
Within a short space I must needs hence.⁺

*Nowadays (offstage).*

The sooner, the liever,⁺ and it be even anon!⁺
I trow⁺ your name is "do little" ye be so long from home,
If ye would go hence, we shall come everychon,⁺
More than a good sort.⁺
Ye have liever,⁺ I dare well say:
To them⁺ ye will, go on your way.
Men have little dainty⁺ of your play,
Because ye make no sport.

---

**ken:** Cause; engender.

**ought:** Perchance; should happen to. In the MS. this reads "owt," which some editors read as "out."

**doctrine:** Teachings; advice.

**set...in heart:** Take to heart.

**I must needs hence:** I will have to go away.

**liever:** Better; more welcome.

**and it be even anon:** Even if it is right away.

**I trow:** I trust; I believe.

**everychon:** Every one.

**sort:** Most likely "circumstance" or "event."

**Ye have liever:** You had better do it. Some editors suggest "Ye have leave," you have permission.

**To them:** Manly (1900) and Furnivall (1904) read this as "to hem"; some later editors have read this as "when." The manuscript is not clear enough for a definitive reading.

**dainty:** Pleasure.

*Nought (offstage).*

> Your pottage* will be for-cold,* sir; when will ye go dine?
> I have seen a man lost twenty nobles* in as little time—
> Yet it was not I, by Saint Quentin.*
> For I was never worth* a potfull of worts* sithen* I was born.
> My name is Nought; I love well to make merry.
> I have be sethe* with the common tapster* of Bury;*
> I played so long the fool, that I am even very weary;
> Yet shall I be there again tomorrow.

---

**pottage:** A soup or stew often eaten by medieval peasants.

**for-cold:** Cold already.

**twenty nobles:** A noble was one of the earliest English gold coins, valued at six shillings and eightpence, or a third of a pre-decimal pound. Twenty nobles (an amount also mentioned in Shakespeare: see 2 Henry IV, act 2, scene 1) would be worth six and two-thirds pounds.

**by Saint Quentin:** The manuscript is unclear here, but most editors agree that the oath is referring to Saint Quentin, an early Christian martyr important in medieval religion. However, Manly (1900) reads this as "by Saint Gis, certain." The medieval name for Quentin, which Furnivall (1904) renders as "Qisyntyn," may have been pronounced very differently than in modern English.

**was never worth:** Never had wealth amounting to.

**worts:** Edible greens; cabbage leaves.

**sithen:** Since.

**be sethe:** The meaning is unclear. The author may mean "sithen," continuously, but since another sense of "sithen" was spelled differently in the previous line, it is more likely some form of "setten," to sit.

**tapster:** Barmaid; at the time, many common tapsters had reputations as less than virtuous women.

**Bury:** Bury St. Edmunds, in Suffolk.

*Mercy.*     I have much care⁺ for you, my own friend;
Your enemies will be here anon;⁺ they made their avaunce.⁺
Think well in your heart your name is Mankind;
Be not unkind to God, I pray you; be his servant,
Be steadfast in condition;⁺ see ye be not variant;⁺
Lose not through folly that is⁺ bought so dear.
God will prove⁺ you soon and, if that you be constant,
Of his bliss perpetual ye shall be partner.

You may not have your intent at your first desire.
See the great patience of Job, and tribulation:
Like as the smith trieth iron in the fire,
So was he tried by God's visitation.⁺
He was of your nature, and of your frailty;
Follow the steps of him, my own sweet son,
And say, as he said, in your trouble and adversity:
*"Dominus dedit, dominus abstulit, sicut sibi placuit; sit nomen Domini benedictum."*⁺

---

**care:** Concern; worry.

**anon:** Soon; immediately.

**avaunce:** This may mean "boast," or it may be an otherwise unrecorded variant of "avauncen," to advance.

**condition:** Character; mode of life.

**variant:** Changeable; contentious; inconsistent.

**that is:** That which is.

**prove:** Test.

**visitation:** Supernatural or divine intervention.

***Dominus dedit, dominus abstulit, sicut sibi placuit; sit nomen Domini benedictum:*** Job's response to adversity, in Job, chapter 1, verse 21: "The Lord gave, and the Lord hath taken away; blessed be the name of the Lord."

Moreover, in special* I give you in charge:
Beware of New Guise, Nowadays, and Nought.
Nice* in their array, in language they be large,*
To pervert thy conditions, all their means shall be sought.
Good son, intermiss* yourself not in their company;
They heard not a mass this twelvemonth, I dare well say.
Give them none audience; they will tell you many a lie;
Do truly your own labour, and keep your holy day.

Beware of Titivillus, for he loseth no way
That goeth invisible and will not be seen;
He will roun* in your ear and cast a net before your eyen.*
He is worst of them all; God let him never theen!*
If ye displease God, ask mercy anon,*
Else Mischief will be ready to brace* you in his bridle.
Kiss me now, my dear darling. God shield you from your fon.*

Do truly your labour, and be never idle.
The blessing of God be with you, and with all your worshipful
 men.

*Exit* MERCY.

---

**in special:** Especially, particularly.

**Nice:** Foolish; ignorant.

**large:** Overgenerous; unrestrained.

**intermiss:** Mingle; be in the midst of. In the manuscript, this has been crossed
 out and "intromitt" (meddle) has been written in another hand.

**roun:** Whisper.

**eyen:** Eyes.

**theen:** Flourish; prosper.

**anon:** Quickly; immediately.

**brace:** Tie up; fetter, as in a horse's harness.

**fon:** Foes; enemies.

*Mankind.*     Amen! For Saint Charity, amen!
               Now blessed be Jesu; my soul is well satiate
               With the mellifluous doctrine of this worshipful man!
               The rebellion of my flesh, now it is superate.*
               Thanked be God of the cunning* that I kan.*
               Here will I sit, and title* in this paper
               The incomparable estate of my promission.*
               Worshipful sovereign, I have written here
               The glorious remembrance of my noble condition.
               To have remorse and memory of myself, thus written it is,
               To defend me from all superstitious charms:
               *"Memento, homo, quod cinis es et cinere reverteris."*＊
               Lo! I bear on my breast the badge of mine arms.

---

**superate:** Conquered; surpassed.

**cunning:** Knowledge; wisdom.

**kan:** Know; am aware of.

**title:** Write down; record.

**promission:** Divine promises.

***Memento, homo, quod cinis es et cinere reverteris:*** "Remember, man, that you
     are dust, and to dust you shall return." A paraphrase of Genesis 3:19,
     used in Ash Wednesday services in Catholic churches.

# Scene 6

*Enter* NEW GUISE *at the back of the stage.*

*New Guise.*  The weather is cold, God send us good feres.⁺
     *Cum sancto sanctus eris,* and *cum perverso perverteris.*\*
     *"Ecce quam bonum et quam jucundum,"* quoth the devil to the
          friars,
     *"Habitare fratres in unum."*\*

*Mankind.*  I hear a fellow speak; with him I will not mell.⁺
     This earth with my spade I shall essay⁺ to delve.⁺
     To eschew⁺ idleness I do it mine own self;
     I pray God send it his foison.⁺

*Enter* NOWADAYS *and* NOUGHT.

*Nowadays.*  Make room, sirs, for we have be long;⁺
     We will come give you a Christmas song.

---

**feres:** Companions.

***Cum sancto sanctus eris,* and *cum perverso perverteris:*** A condensed
    quotation from 2 Samuel 22:26-27; the sense is, "With the holy you will
    be holy...with the perverse, perverted."

***Ecce quam bonum et quam jucundum...habitare fratres in unum:*** The
    beginning of Psalm 133: "Behold how good it is and how pleasant for
    brothers to dwell together in unity."

**mell:** Speak.

**essay:** Try, attempt.

**delve:** Dig.

**eschew:** Avoid.

**foison:** Abundance; plenty.

**we have be long:** The meaning is unclear; possibly Nowadays is commenting
    that they have been away for too long.

*Nought.* Now I pray all the yeomandry that is here
To sing with us with a merry cheer:

*He sings:** 

It is written with a coal, it is written with a coal

*Nowadays and New-Guise.*
It is written with a coal, it is written with a coal

*Nought.* He that shitteth with his hole, he that shitteth with his hole

*Nowadays and New-Guise.*
He that shitteth with his hole, he that shitteth with his hole

*Nought.* But⁺ he wipe his arse clean, but he wipe his arse clean

*Nowadays and New-Guise.*
But he wipe his arse clean, but he wipe his arse clean

*Nought.* On his breech⁺ it shall be seen, on his breech it shall be seen.

*Nowadays and New-Guise.*
On his breech it shall be seen, on his breech it shall be seen.

*All sing.* Holyke,⁺ holyke, holyke; holyke, holyke, holyke!

---

**He sings:** As they repeat each line, Nowadays and New Guise encourage the audience to sing along.

**But:** Unless.

**breech:** Undergarment covering the buttocks.

**Holyke:** Evidently a nonsense word, and more than likely some sort of obscure scatological pun, possibly involving "hol-leke," an obsolete name for a scallion. Bruster and Rasmussen (2009), following a previous edition by Mark Eccles, suggests "hole-lick."

*New Guise.*   Ey, Mankind, God speed you with your spade!
　　　　　I shall tell you of a marriage:
　　　　　I would your mouth, and his arse that this made,
　　　　　Were married junctly* together.

*Mankind.*   Hie you hence, fellows, with braiding!*
　　　　　Leave your derision and your japing.
　　　　　I must needs labour; it is my living.

*Nowadays.*   What, sir? We came but late* hither.
　　　　　Shall all this* corn grow here
　　　　　That ye shall have the next year?
　　　　　If it be so, corn had need be dear,*
　　　　　Else ye shall have a poor life.

*Nought.*   Alas, poor father! This labour fretteth* you to the bone,
　　　　　But for your crop, I take great moan.*
　　　　　Ye shall never spend it alone;
　　　　　I shall assay to get you a wife.
　　　　　How many acres suppose ye here, by estimation?

*New Guise.*   Ey, how ye turn the earth up and down!
　　　　　I have be* in my days in many good town,
　　　　　Yet saw I never such another tilling!

*Mankind.*   Why stand ye idle? It is pity that ye were born.

---

**junctly:** Jointly.

**braiding:** Upbraiding; reproach. The manuscript has "bredyng."

**late:** Recently; lately.

**all this:** Here carries the sense of "all of the."

**dear:** Expensive; valuable.

**fretteth:** Injures or devours.

**take great moan:** Make great lamentation.

**have be:** Have been.

*Nowadays.*　We shall bargain with you, and neither mock nor scorn.
　　　　　Take a good cart in harvest and load it with your corn,
　　　　　And what shall we give you for the leaving?*

*Nought.*　He is a good stark* labourer; he would fain* do well;
　　　　　He hath met with the good man Mercy in a shrewed sell.*
　　　　　For all this, he may have many a hungry meal;
　　　　　Yet well ye see, he is politic.*
　　　　　Here shall be good corn, he may not miss it;
　　　　　If he will have rain, he may over-piss* it;
　　　　　And if he will have compost, he may over-bliss* it
　　　　　A little with his arse, like.

*Mankind.*　Go and do your labour; God let you never theen!*
　　　　　Or with my spade I shall you ding,* by the holy trinity!
　　　　　Have ye none other man to mock, but ever me?
　　　　　Ye would have me of your set?
　　　　　Hie you forth lively, for hence I will you drive!

　　　　　　　MANKIND *beats them with his spade.*

---

**leaving:** Here, gleanings, remnants of the harvest picked from the fields by the
　　　poor, usually free of charge.

**stark:** Strong; sturdy.

**would fain:** Would gladly; would be pleased to.

**in a shrewed sell:** At an unlucky moment.

**politic:** Wise; well-governed.

**over-piss:** Urinate upon.

**over-bliss:** Bless or consecrate.

**theen:** Flourish; prosper.

**ding:** Beat; beat up.

*New Guise.*   Alas, my jewels!* I shall be shent of* my wife!

*Nowadays.*   Alas! and I am like never for to thrive,*
              I have such a buffet!*

*Mankind.*    Hence, I say, New Guise, Nowadays, and Nought!
              It was said before, all the means should be sought
              To pervert my conditions* and bring me to nought.
              Hence, thieves, ye have made many a lesing!*

*Nought.*     Merde!* I was for-cold,* but now am I warm!
              Ye are evil* advised, sir, for ye have done harm.
              By Cock's body sacred,* I have such a pain in my arm
              I may not change a man a farthing!

*Mankind.*    Now I thank God, kneeling on my knee.
              Blessed be his name, he is of high degree!

---

**jewels:** Testicles.

**shent of:** Shamed or disgraced with respect to.

**thrive:** Prosper; flourish; grow older.

**I have such a buffet:** I have received such a blow.

**conditions:** Character; situation in life.

**lesing:** Lies; destruction. The same word is also used for gleanings.

**Merde:** Manly (1897) and Furnivall and Pollard (1904) give this word as "Marryde." The manuscript is unclear, but an oath or exclamation seems more likely, such as this word, meaning excrement, which was subsequently lost to English, then borrowed again as a French loan-word.

**for-cold:** Very cold.

**evil:** Badly; wrongly.

**By Cock's body sacred:** A minced oath.

By the feoffs* of his grace that he hath sent me,
Three of mine enemies I have put to flight.
Yet this instrument, sovereigns, is not made to defend.
David sayeth: *Nec in hasta, nec in gladio salvat Dominus.*\*

*Nought.*  No, marry, I beshrew* you, it is *in spadibus.*\*
Therefore, Christ's curse come on your *headibus,*\*
To send you less might!

*Exit* NEW GUISE, NOWADAYS, *and* NOUGHT.

*Mankind.*  I promitt* you, these fellows will no more come here,
For some of them, certainly, were somewhat too near.
My father, Mercy, advised me to be of a good cheer,
And against my enemies manly for to fight.
I shall convict* them, I hope, everychon*—

---

**feoffs:** Benefits with which one may be invested; a legal term. The MS is unclear; Manly (1897) reads it as "By the fesyde," which he corrects to "By this spade;" Furnivall and Pollard (1904) have "By the syde" and also suggest "By the ayde."

***Nec in hasta, nec in gladio salvat Dominus:*** A paraphrase of 1 Samuel 17:47: "the Lord saves not with sword and spear."

**beshrew:** Curse.

***in spadibus...headibus*:** Nought's faux-Latin for "spade" and "head" mocks Mankind's Latin quotation. Not a reference to the modern expression "in spades," a twentieth century coinage.

**promitt:** Promise.

**convict:** Defeat; vanquish; overcome.

**everychon:** Every one.

Yet I say amiss: I do it not alone.
With the help of the grace of God, I resist my foen*
And their malicious hurt.
With my spade I will depart, my worshipful sovereigns,
And live ever with labour to correct my insolence.
I shall go fett* corn for my land; I pray you of patience;*
Right soon I shall revert.*

*Exit* MANKIND.

---

**foen:** Foes.

**fett:** Fetch; obtain.

**I pray you of patience:** I ask you to have patience.

**revert:** Return.

# Scene 7

*Enter* MISCHIEF.

Mischief.   Alas, alas, that ever I was wrought!
Alas the while,* I am worse than nought!
Sithen* I was here, by Him that me bought,
I am utterly undone!
I, Mischief, was here at the beginning of the game,
And argued with Mercy; God give him shame!
He hath taught Mankind, while I have be wane,*
To fight manly against his foen;*
For with his spade, that was his weapon,
New Guise, Nowadays, Nought, hath all to-beaten.*
I have great pity to see them weeping.
Will ye list?* I hear them cry.

*Enter* NEW GUISE, NOWADAYS, *and* NOUGHT.

Mischief.   Alas, alas! Come hither; I shall be your borrow.*
Alack, alack! *Veni, veni!** Come hither, with sorrow!
Peace, fair babies! Ye shall have an apple tomorrow!
Why grete* ye so, why?

---

**Alas the while:** Alas for the current state of circumstances.

**Sithen:** Since.

**be wane:** Been lacking.

**foen:** Foes.

**to-beaten:** Badly beaten. A word is likely missing here, indicating that Mankind is the one who has beaten them.

**list:** Listen.

**borrow:** Ransom; redeemer.

***Veni, veni*:** Come, come. Used in the Latin hymn "Veni, veni, Emmanuel."

**grete:** Weep; lament.

*New Guise.* Alas, master! Alas, my privity!*

*Mischief.* Ah, where? Alack! Fair babe, ba* me!
Abide;* too soon I shall it see.

*Nowadays.* Here, here! See my head, good master!

*Mischief.* Lady, help! Silly darling, ven, ven!*
I shall help thee of thy pain;
I shall smite off thy head, and set it on again!

*Nought.* By our lady, sir, a fair plaster.*
Will ye off with his head? it is a shrewd* charm.
As for me, I have none* harm.
I were loath to forbear* mine arm.
Ye play:* *in nomine patris,* chop!

*New Guise.* Ye shall not chop my jewels, an I may!

*Nowadays.* Ye, Christ's cross! Will ye smite my head away?
There? Where? On, anon!* Out! Ye shall not assay;
I might well be called a fop!*

---

**privity:** Genitals.

**ba:** Kiss.

**Abide:** Wait; hold on.

**ven:** Come.

**fair plaster:** Good medicine.

**shrewd:** Wicked; evil.

**none:** no.

**forbear:** Give up; relinquish.

**play:** Do thusly.

**On, anon:** Thus in Manly (1900); Furnivall (1904) suggests "On and on."

**fop:** Fool; the word had not yet acquired its later association with vanity and dandyism.

*Mischief.*   I can chop it off, and make it again.

*New Guise.*   I had a shrewd recumbentibus,˙ but I feel no pain.

*Nowadays.*   And my head is all safe and whole again.
Now, touching the matter of Mankind,
Let us have an interlection,˙ sithen˙ he be come hither:
It were good to have an end.

*Mischief.*   How, how! A minstrel! Know ye any ought?

*Nought.*   I can pipe in a Walsingham whistle,˙ I, Nought, Nought.

*Mischief.*   Blow apace; thou shall bring him in with a flute.

*Titivillus (offstage).*\*
I come, with my legs under me!

*Mischief.*   How, New Guise, Nowadays, hark, or I go:
When our heads were together I spake of "*si dedero.*"˙

---

**recumbentibus:** A knock-down blow.

**interlection:** Discussion; conference.

**sithen:** Since.

**Walsingham whistle:** Some have suggested this refers to flutes played by
pilgrims to Walsingham.

**offstage:** The MS stage direction reads, "shouts outside."

**_si dedero:_** The reference is to a satirical Latin song consisting of a series of
couplets, the first line of each couplet beginning with "Si dedero,"
meaning "If I give..." and the second beginning with "Ni dedero...,"
discussing what should be received in return. The implication is that for
everything you give, you should receive something in return; New Guise
takes the hint and starts collecting money from the audience.

*New Guise.*  Yo! Go thy way! We shall gather money⁺ unto;⁺
Else they shall no man him see.⁺
Now ghostly to our purpose,⁺ worshipful sovereigns!
We intend to gather money, if it please your negligence,
For a man with a head that is⁺ of great omnipotence.⁺

*Nowadays.*  Keep your taille,⁺ in goodness I pray you, good brother.
He is a worshipfull man, sirs, saving your reverence;
He loveth no groats,⁺ nor pence or twopence;
Give us red royals⁺ if you will see his abominable presence!

*New Guise.*  Not so! Ye that mow⁺ not pay the ton,⁺ pay the tother.⁺
At the goodman⁺ of this house first we will assay.⁺

---

**We shall gather money:** See the Introduction and Appendixes regarding the collection of money during the performance.

**unto:** Therefore; for that purpose.

**they shall no man him see:** Nobody will see him, referring to Titivillus.

**ghostly to our purpose:** Let us get down seriously to business.

**that is:** The manuscript reads "that."

**great omnipotence:** As in modern English, omnipotent means "all-powerful;" this is a comic overstatement by New Guise.

**taille:** Tally; account of income. "Tayll" in the manuscript.

**groats:** Coins worth four pence each.

**red royals:** Golden ("red") coins worth ten shillings, also known as "rose nobles."

**mow:** Are able to; may.

**ton...tother:** One...other.

**goodman:** Person in charge, head of household; here, most likely, the proprietor of the inn-yard where the play was being performed.

**assay:** Make an attempt.

God bless you, master! You say us ill,⁺ yet ye will not say nay.
Let us go by and by,⁺ and do them pay;
Ye pay all alike; well must ye fare!

*Nought.*        I say, New Guise, Nowadays: *"Esits vos pecuniatus?"*⁺
I have cried⁺ a fair while; I beshrew your *patus.*⁺

*Nowadays.*   *Ita vere, magister;*⁺ come forth now your *gatus.*⁺
He is a goodly⁺ man, sirs; make space, and beware!

---

**say us ill:** Speak ill of us.

**by and by:** Here and there.

***Estis vos pecuniatus:*** Dog-Latin for "Are you moneyed," or "Do you have any money."

**cried:** Shouted; begged.

**beshrew your *patus*:** Curse your head.

***Ita vere, magister:*** It is so, master.

**your *gatus*:** From your gates; alternately, using another sense of "gate," this could be read as "on your way."

**goodly:** Excellent; handsome; large in size.

# Scene 8

*Enter* TITIVILLUS, *dress'd like a devil, and with a net in his hand.*

Titivillus.     *Ego sum dominancium dominus,*⁺ and my name is Titivillus.
                Ye that have good horse, to you I say, "*caveatis.*"⁺
                Here is an able fellowship to trice⁺ him out at your gates.

                *(to* NEW GUISE*).*

                *Ego probo sic:*⁺ Sir New Guise, lend me a penny!

New Guise.     I have a great purse, sir, but I have no money.
                By the Mass, I fail two farthings of an halfpenny.⁺
                Yet had I ten pound this night that was.

*Titivillus (to Nowadays).*

                What is in thy purse? Thou art a stout⁺ fellow.

Nowadays.      The devil have the quill,⁺ I am a clean⁺ gentleman.
                I pray God, I be never worse stored⁺ than I am;
                It shall be otherwise, I hope, or this night pass.

---

***Ego sum dominancium dominus:*** I am the Lord of Lords.

***caveatis:*** Beware.

**trice:** Snatch.

***Ego probo sic:*** I will prove it; I will prove it thusly.

**I fail two farthings of an halfpenny:** A farthing was a quarter of a penny, so two farthings less than a halfpenny was nothing at all.

**stout:** Mighty; noble; excellent; strong.

**devil have the quill:** The meaning is unclear. Some later editors (Bruster and Rasmussen, 2009) have suggested "whit" for "quill."

**clean:** Empty-handed.

**stored:** Provisioned; provided for.

*Titivillus (to Nought).*
        Hark, now! I say thou hast many a penny?

*Nought.*     *Non nobis, domine;* non nobis,* by Saint Denis!
        The devil may dance in my purse for any penny;
        It is as clean as a bird's arse.

*Titivillus.*    Now I say again, *caveatis!*
        Here is an able fellowship to trice him of your gates.
        Now I say, New Guise, Nowadays, and Nought,
        Go and search the country, anon that it be sought;*
        Some here, some there; what if ye may catch ought?
        If ye fail of horse, take what ye may else.

*New Guise.* Then speak to Mankind, for the recumbentibus* of my jewels.

*Nowadays.* Remember my broken head in the worship of the five
            volailles.*

*Nought.*     Yea, good sir, by the sciatica in my arm.

*Titivillus.*    I know full well what Mankind did to you;
        Mischief hath informed of all the matter through.
        I shall venge* your quarrel; I made God a vow.
        Forth, and espy where ye may do harm.

---

**Non nobis, domine:** The first line of a traditional Latin canon hymn of
thanksgiving; "Not us, Lord."

**anon that it be sought:** That it (the horse) might be looked for immediately.

**recumbentibus:** Hard blow; literally, a knock-down blow.

**five volailles:** Five fowls (?). The MS. here is unclear but appears to be
something like "x volvollys" or "v voliellys." Manly (1900) gives it as "v
voli ellys;" Furnivall (1904) gives "vowellys." Both suggest some
variation of "the seven (or twenty) devils." Likely a minced oath, some
variation of "by Christ's five wounds."

**venge:** Avenge; repay.

Take William Fyde,* if ye will have any more.
I say, New Guise, whither art thou avised* to go?

*New Guise.* First I shall begin at Master Huntington of Sanston,
From thence, I shall go to William Thurlay of Hanston,
And so forth to Pycharde of Trumpington.
I will keep me to these three.

*Nowadays.* I shall go to William Baker of Walton,
To Richard Bollman of Gayton;
I shall spare Master Wood of Fullburn;
He is a *"noli me tangere!"**

*Nought.* I shall go to William Patrick of Massingham;
I shall spare Master Allington of Botysam,
And Hammond of Soffeham.
Fellows, come forth, and go we hence together;
For dread of *in manus tuas,* quack!*

---

**William Fyde:** According to Bruster and Rasmussen (2009), this, along with the names listed in the next three lines, consist, at least so far as they can be identified, "with individuals living in and around Cambridgeshire and Norfolk during the period Mankind was composed." They would have to be public figures to allow the local in-jokes to be appreciated. The structure of this and the following passage suggest that the names may have been switched around, either to allow for changes in local news and gossip, or when the traveling players presented this piece in other parts of England.

**avised:** Inclined; intending.

*noli me tangere:* Don't touch me. This is another Biblical reference; they are words spoken by Jesus to Mary Magdalene after his resurrection, according to the Gospel of John.

*in manus tuas,* **quack:** In manus tuas is another Biblical quote, the last words of Jesus according to the Gospel of Luke. It was, according to Smart (1916), frequently heard at public executions, both by the priest giving the criminal last rites and frequently spoken by the prisoner as his or her own last words, and so came to stand for an execution generally. The final word is given as "qweke" in both Manly (1900) and Furnivall (1904); it is a conventional early onomatopoeia for the sound made by a duck or goose; as seen later in the play, it is also used to refer to the sound made by a person being hanged or strangled.

*New Guise.* Sith⁺ we shall go, let us be well ware and wither;⁺
If we may be take, we come no more hither.
Let us con⁺ well over neck-verse⁺ that we have not a check.⁺

*Titivillus.* Go your way, a devil way,⁺ go your way, all.
I bless you with my left hand;⁺ foul you befall!⁺
Come again, I warn, as soon as I you call,
And bring your advantage⁺ into this place.
To speak with Mankind I will tarry here this tide,⁺
And assay⁺ his good purpose for to set aside.
The good man, Mercy, shall no longer be his guide;
I shall make him to dance another trace!⁺

---

**sith:** Since.

**ware and wither:** well-informed and forceful or ferocious.

**con:** Study.

**neck-verse:** In early medieval England, priests could be transferred out of the jurisdiction of secular courts to the ecclesiastical courts by demonstrating the ability to read and interpret scripture. Where secular courts often punished crimes harshly, with hanging for many crimes, in the ecclesiastical court you might escape the same crime with only a pennance. By the time Mankind was written, this privilege had been extended to any person who could prove they could read a passage from the Bible. Because the same passage was almost always chosen, the first line of Psalm 51, some illiterate people would memorize this "neck verse" instead.

**check:** Setback; in this case, being hanged.

**a devil way:** A common emphatic way of saying "away".

**bless you with my left hand:** The left hand was associated with wickedness in contemporary superstition.

**foul you befall:** Commit acts of wickedness.

**advantage:** Profits; spoils.

**this tide:** For a little while.

**assay:** Try; make an attempt.

**dance another trace:** Change his attitude.

*Exit all but* TITIVILLUS.*

| | |
|---|---|
| *Titivillus.* | Ever I go invisible; it is my jet;*<br>And before his eyes, thus, I will hang my net<br>To blench* his sight. I hope to have his foot met.*<br>To irk him of his labour* I shall make a frame.*<br>This board shall be hid under the earth privily;*<br>His spade shall enter, I hope, unreadily.*<br>By then he hath assayed,* he shall be very angry<br>And lose his patience, pain of shame.*<br>I shall menge* his corn* with drawk and with darnel;*<br>It shall not be like* to sow nor to sell. |

---

**Exit all but Titivillus:** The manuscript does not indicate where in this speech the three minor devils exit. Many editors have them leave four lines earlier, after Titivillus stops addressing them directly.

**jet:** Habit or custom.

**blench:** Avoid; deceive; mislead.

**met:** Measured; here, may also imply "caught."

**irk him of his labour:** Make him tired of or annoyed with his work.

**make a frame:** Receive a benefit; also, as a pun, to build a structure, especially a gallows.

**privily:** Secretly.

**unreadily:** Not easily.

**By then he hath assayed:** By the time he has finished his attempt (to dig through the board).

**pain of shame:** Or I will be ashamed; Bruster and Rasmussen (2009) identify this as a mild oath also found in other plays of the period.

**menge:** Mix.

**corn:** Generally, grain; here, the seed grain Mankind is attempting to sow.

**drawk...darnel:** Common weeds found in fields of cereal grains.

**like:** Suitable.

Yonder he cometh! I pray of counsel.*
He shall ween* grace were wane.*

---

**pray of counsel:** Ask you to keep this secret.

**ween:** Believe; the word implies that the belief is false.

**wane:** Dwindling; disappearing.

# Scene 9

*Enter* MANKIND.

*Mankind.*    Now God, of his mercy, send us of his sonde.<sup>*</sup>
I have brought seed here to sow with my land.<sup>*</sup>
While I overdelve<sup>*</sup> it, here it shall stand.

MANKIND *sets down his seed and begins to work the ground;* TITIVILLUS *steals the seed.*

*Mankind.*    *In nomine Patris et Filii et Spiritus Santi.*<sup>*</sup> Now I will begin.
This land is so hard, it maketh unlusty<sup>*</sup> and irk.<sup>*</sup>
I shall sow my corn at winter and let God work.
Alas, my corn is lost! Here is a foul work.
I see well, by tilling little shall I win.
Here I give up my spade, for now and for ever.

*Here* TITIVILLUS *goeth out with the spade.*

---

**sonde:** Here, God's grace; may also refer to a gift, mission or commandment from God.

**to sow with my land:** To sow in my land; to sow my land with.

**overdelve:** Dig in the ground; here, to prepare furrows for planting the seed.

***In nomine Patris et Filii et Spiritus Santi:*** In the name of the father, and the son, and the holy spirit; a common Christian ejaculation.

**unlusty:** Lazy; slothful; dull.

**irk:** Tired; vexed; weary.

*Mankind.*   To occupy my body, I will not put me in dever.*
             I will hear my evensong* here, or I dissever.*
             This place I assign as for my kirk;*
             Here, in my kirk, I kneel on my knees.
             *Pater noster, qui es in celis...*

TITIVILLUS *re-enters.*

*Titivillus.*   I promise you, I have no lead on my heels;
                I am here again to make this fellow irk.
                Whist! Peace!* I shall go to his ear and titill* therein.

*(to* MANKIND*)*

A short prayer thrilleth* heaven; of thy prayer blin;*
Thou art holier than ever was any of thy kin.
Arise and avent* thee! Nature compells.

---

**put me in dever:** take personal responsibility; make an effort.

**evensong:** Liturgical prayers, often sung, which took place in the late afternoon or early evening; here, Mankind's evening prayers.

**or I dissever:** The sense seems to be "before I depart."

**kirk:** Church.

*Pater noster....:* The beginning of the Lord's Prayer.

**Whist! Peace!:** Be quiet!

**titill:** Whisper; gossip; tattle.

**thrilleth:** Penetrates to; perforates.

**blin:** Stop; give up; be silent; bring to an end.

**avent:** Air out; come out; escape into the open air.

*Mankind.*  I will into this yard, sovereigns, and come again soon,
For dread of the colic,* and eke* of the stone.*
I will go do that needs must be done;
My beads* shall be here, for whosoever will come.

*Exit* MANKIND.

*Titivillus.*  Mankind was busy in his prayers, yet I did him arise.*
He is conveyed, by Christ,* from his divine service.
Whither is he, trow ye? I wisse,* I am wonder wise;*
I have sent him forth to shit lesings.*
If ye have any silver, in hap* pure brass,
Take a little powder of Paris* and cast over* his face,
And even in the owl-flight* let him pass;
Titivillus can learn you many pretty things!

---

**colic...stone:** Colic is a disease of the colon and lower intestine; stone is a disease of the kidney or bladder. Mankind is interrupting his prayers to relieve himself ("nature compels") to avoid illness.

**eke:** also.

**beads:** Prayer beads.

**did him arise:** Made him get up; made him stop.

**by Christ:** An exclamation or oath, not an indication of agency.

**I wisse:** Literally, I make it known; here, the sense seems to be along the lines of "I tell you."

**wonder wise:** Extraordinarily wise.

**lesings:** Lies or falsehood; to make lesings was to tell lies.

**in hap:** Perhaps.

**powder of Paris:** Plaster of paris; gypsum plaster.

**cast over:** Make a cast or copy of.

**owl-flight:** Fitzgerald and Sebastian (2012) suggest "the dark."

I trow* Mankind will come again soon,
Or else, I fear me, evensong will be done;
His beads shall be triced* aside, and that anon.*
Ye shall see a good sport, if ye will abide;*
Mankind cometh again. Well fare he!
I shall answer him *ad omnia quare.**
There shall be set abroach* a clerical* matter;
I hope of his purpose to set him aside.*

*Re-enter* MANKIND.

*Mankind.*    Evensong hath been in the saying, I trow, a fair while;*
I am irk of* it; it is too long, by one mile.
Do way!* I will no more so oft on the church stile;*

---

**I trow:** I trust; I believe.

**triced:** Pushed. This is the most plausible reading of the manuscript's "trysyd."

**anon:** Quickly; immediately.

**abide:** Stay; remain.

*ad omnia quare:* With an answer for every question.

**set abroach:** Broached (in conversation); Titivillus is saying that there will be a discussion started on the subject. Literally, to tap or open a hole in a barrel of wine or beer.

**clerical:** Learned.

**set him aside:** Here, the sense is to lead him astray (from his purpose).

**hath been in the saying, I trow, a fair while:** Has, I think, been going on for a long time.

**irk of:** Annoyed with.

**do way:** Stop it.

**church stile:** The gate or way to the church. A stile could be a step leading over a wall or a narrow gap between fences; it was designed to allow people to cross a boundary without allowing animals through. Here, it is used as a synechdoche for the church itself.

Be as be may,\* I shall do another;
Of labour and prayer, I am near irk of\* both;
I will no more of it, though Mercy be wroth.\*
My head is very heavy, I tell you for sooth;\*
I shall sleep full my belly,\* an he was\* my brother.

*Titivillus (to the audience).*
And ever ye did,\* keep now your silence!
Not a word, I charge you, pain of\* forty pence!
A pretty\* game shall be showed you, or\* ye go hence.
Ye may hear him snore; he is sad\* asleep.
Whist! Peace!\* The devil is dead. I shall go round in his ear.

---

**Be as be may:** Whatever happens. In the manuscript, this line and the
following two are inserted as a note at the bottom of the page;
presumably the copyist skipped them inadvertently.

**irk of:** Annoyed with.

**wroth:** Angry.

**for sooth:** Truly; honestly.

**full my belly:** Here, the sense seems to be that Mankind will sleep until he is
satisfied or has had as much sleep as he wants.

**an he was:** Even if he were.

**An ever ye did:** If you ever did.

**pain of:** On pain of; or risk a penalty of.

**pretty:** Cunning; wily; skillful.

**or:** Before.

**sad:** Soundly; deeply.

**Whist! Peace!:** Be quiet!

TITIVILLUS *whispers in* MANKIND'S *ear.*

*Titivillus.*    Alas, Mankind, alas! Mercy stown* a mare!
          He is run away from his master, there wot* no man where!
          Moreover, he stole both a horse and a neat.*
          But yet I heard say he brake* his neck as he rode in France;
          But I think he rideth over the gallows, to learn how to dance,
          Because of this theft; that is his governance.*
          Trust no more on him: he is a marred man.
          Mickle* sorrow with thy spade before thou hast wrought;
          Arise and ask mercy of New Guise, Nowadays, and Nought.
          They come; advise thee for the best, let their good will be
                sought,
          And thy own wife brethel,* and take thee a lemman.*

*(Aside)*

          Farewell, everychon,* for I have done my game;
          For I have brought Mankind to mischief and to shame.

*Exit* TITIVILLUS.

---

**stown:** Stole; has stolen.

**wot:** Knows.

**neat:** A domestic animal; usually a head of cattle or an ox.

**brake:** Broke.

**governance:** Authority; method of influence.

**Mickle:** Much.

**brethel:** Most modern editions follow Manly (1900) in suggesting "brethel," betray, for what Manly read as "brechell." Furnivall and Pollard (1904) suggest "be thell," be left. The original manuscript is not clear enough to judge with confidence, but the sense of the line is clear from context.

**lemman:** Mistress.

**everychon:** Every one.

# Scene 10

MANKIND *alone.*

*Mankind.*  Whoop! Whoo! Mercy hath broken his neckercher,\* a vows,\*
Or he hangeth by his neck high up on the gallows.
Adieu, fair master! I will haste me to the ale-house,
And speak with New Guise, Nowadays, and Nought—
And get me a lemman\* with a smattering\* face!

*Enter* NEW GUISE.

*New Guise.*  Make space! For Cock's body sacred, make space!
A-ha! Well! On! Run! God give him evil grace!
We were near Saint Patrick's way, by him that me bought;
I was twitched\* by the neck; the game was begun;
A grace was,\* the halter\* brast\* asunder—*ecce signum,*\*
The half is about my neck. We had a near run!
"Beware," quoth the goodwife, when she smote off her
husband's head, "beware!"

---

**neckercher:** Literally a neckerchief; here referring to Mercy's neck.

**a vows:** The meaning is unclear, but likely along the lines of "I vow" or "he vows."

**lemman:** Mistress.

**smattering:** The likely meaning is attractive, possibly with an implication of wantonness or unseemliness.

**twitched:** Hanged.

**A grace was:** By a lucky chance.

**halter:** Noose.

**brast:** Burst.

*ecce signum:* Look at the proof, in this case the noose around New Guise's neck.

Mischief is a convict, for he could his neck-verse.\*
My body gave a swing when I hung upon the case.\*
Alas, he will hang such a lightly\* man and a fierce
For stealing of an horse, I pray God give him care.
Do way\* this halter! What devil doth Mankind here, with
    sorrow?
Alas, how my neck is sore, I make avow!

*Mankind.*    Ye be welcome, New Guise. Sir, what cheer with you?

*New Guise.*   Well, sir, I have no cause to mourn.

*Mankind.*    What was there about your neck? So God you amend!\*

*New Guise.*   In faith, Saint Audrey's holy band;\*

---

**a convict, for he could his neck-verse:** For neck-verse, see note to scene 8. It is unclear whether Mercy is a prisoner of the ecclesiastical authorities because he successfully read the verse, or if he was convicted "fore" (before) he could do so. Somerset (2013) suggests "conned," learned by heart, for "could."

**hung upon the case:** "Case" can refer to a box, a coffin, or a chance or event; to hang upon the case might suggest awaiting the final event. Other editors suggest that "case" refers to the gibbet or gallows, which makes sense in context.

**lightly:** The manuscript is obscure but seems to read "lyghly." The intended meaning might be easygoing, ready, quick, or insignificant; or it could be some variation of "likely," meaning good-looking.

**Do way:** Away with.

**amend:** Recover; get better.

**Saint Audrey's holy band:** Saint Audrey of Ely, also known as Etheldreda, was an East Anglian abbess and queen. She died of a buboe or tumor on her neck, which was said to be punishment for wearing showy and expensive necklaces before becoming a nun. Silk and lace necklaces were later sold at St. Audrey's Fair, most of which were of poor quality; as a result, St. Audrey, later shortened to "tawdry," was used to describe shoddy workmanship. Here, New Guise pretends that the noose he was wearing around his neck was one of these lace necklaces, which he was wearing in an attempt to cure himself of a disease of the neck.

I have a little disease,* as it please God to send,
With a running ringworm.*

*Enter* NOWADAYS.

*Nowadays.* Stand a room,* I pray thee, brother mine;
I have laboured all this night, when shall we go dine?
A church here beside shall pay for ale, bread, and wine;
Lo! Here is stuff* will serve.

*New Guise.* Now, by the holy Mary, thou art better merchant than I!

*Enter* NOUGHT.

*Nought.* Avaunt,* knaves, let me go by!
I cannot get* and I should starve.

*Enter* MISCHIEF, *with fetters on his arms.*

*Mischief.* Here cometh a man of arms; why stand you so still?
Of murder and manslaughter I have my belly full.

*Nowadays.* What, Mischief, have ye been in prison, and it be your will?
Me seemeth* ye have scoured a pair of fetters.*

---

**disease:** Discomfort; suffering.

**running ringworm:** A skin disease; Bruster and Rasmussen (2009) suggest tinea sycosis or tinea circinata.

**Stand a room:** Give me room; stand aside.

**stuff:** Supplies, provisions.

**avaunt:** Move.

**get:** Most modern editors follow Furnivall and Pollard (1904), who give this word as "geet." However, Manly (1900) gives it as "gret," to cry or lament.

**me seemeth:** It seems to me.

**scoured a pair of fetters:** Farmer (1909) describes this as "a very common piece of Old Cant," or prison slang, meaning to wear fetters on the hands. The maunscript reads "scoryde;" it is also possible this should be read as "scored," cut off.

*Mischief.*     I was chained by the arms; lo, I have them here.
              The chains I brast* asunder, and killed the jailer.
              Yea, and his fair wife halsed* in a corner.
              Ah! How sweetly I kissed that sweet mouth of hers!
              When I had do, I was mine own butler;
              I brought away with me both dish and doubler.*
              Here is enow* for me; be of good cheer.
              Yet well fare the new chesaunce!*

*Mankind.*     I ask mercy of New Guise, Nowadays, and Nought.
              Once, with my spade, I remember that I fought;
              I will make you amends if I hurt you ought,
              Or did any grievance.*

*New Guise.*   What a devil liketh ye* to be of this disposition?

*Mankind.*     I dreamt Mercy was hang'd—this was my vision—
              And that to you three I should have recourse and remotion.*
              Now I pray you heartily, of your good will,
              I cry you mercy of all that I did amiss.

*Nowadays (aside).*
              I say, New Guise, Nought—Titivillus made all this;
              As secure as God is in heaven, so it is!

---

**brast:** Burst.

**halsed:** Embraced; caressed.

**doubler:** Platter. Colloquially, "dish and doubler" or "dish, pan, and doubler" refers to all of a person's belongings, or all of a home's contents.

**enow:** Enough.

**chesaunce:** Acquisition; sustenance; outcome; may also refer to borrowed money.

**grievance:** Injury; offense; annoyance.

**What a devil liketh thee:** Why on earth are you inclined.

**remotion:** Going back to; falling back on.

*Nought.*   Stand up on your feet! Why stand you so still?

*New Guise.*   Master Mischief, we will you exhort
Mankind's name in your book for to report.

*Mischief.*   I will not do so; I will sit a court.*
Nowadays, make proclamation,*
And* do it *forma juris,** dasart!*

*Nowadays.*   Oyez! Oyez! Oyez!
All manner of men, and common women,
To the court of Mischief come or send;
Mankind shall return, he is one of our men.

*Mischief.*   Nought, come forth; thou shall be steward.

*New Guise.*   Master Mischief, his side gown* may be torde;*
He may have a jacket thereof and money told.*

---

**sit a court:** Hold a court session (as a judge).

**Nowadays, make proclamation:** In the manuscript, this line appears to the right, between Michief's other two lines. Manly (1900) interprets this as a stage direction; most modern editors consider it part of Mischief's line.

**and:** The manuscript reads "A."

**forma juris:** In proper legal form.

**dasart:** Dullard.

**side gown:** "Side" in this case probably means long or voluminous; a gown made of much fabric.

**torde:** This word is unclear in the manuscript, and later editors disagree on what it might represent. Manly (1900) thinks it reads "tolde" but suggests it should be "solde;" Furnivall thinks the manuscript reads "solde." Another possibility, adopted here, is that this is some form of the Middle English verb "torenden" or "todelen," both of which can mean "to tear" or "to divide up."

**told:** Paid out; returned. The idea is that Mankind may cut a jacket out of his long gown, and sell the rest of the cloth for a profit.

54

NOUGHT writes.*

| | |
|---|---|
| *Mankind.* | I will do for the best, so I have no cold.*<br>Hold, I pray you, and take it with you,<br>And let me have it again in any wise.* |
| *New Guise.* | I promitt* you a fresh* jacket, after the new guise.* |
| *Mankind.* | Go and do that longeth to your office,*<br>And spare that ye mow!* |

Exit NEW GUISE with MANKIND'S jacket.

| | |
|---|---|
| *Nought.* | Hold, master Mischief, and read this! |
| *Mischief.* | Here is blottibus in blottis,<br>Blottorum blottibus istis.*<br>Beshrew* your eyes, a fair hand! |

---

**Nought writes:** In the manuscript, "Nought scr" appears at the edge of the page next to Mankind's line following, with the remaining cut off. Manly (1900) suggests "scribit." Furnivall (1904) instead suggests that this indicates that the last two lines of the following speech are spoken by Nought, rather than by Mankind, a suggestion little followed by later editors.

**so I have no cold:** So long as I am not, or (possibly) do not get, cold.

**in any wise:** Somehow; in some form; by some means.

**promitt:** Promise; pledge.

**fresh:** New.

**guise:** Fashion.

**that longeth to your office:** That that is proper to your role or function.

**that ye mow:** Whatever you can.

***blottibus in blottis...:*** Nonsense Latin, indicating messy (blotted) handwriting.

**Beshrew:** Curse; damn.

| | |
|---|---|
| *Nowadays.* | Yea, it is a good running fist;* |
| | Such an hand may not be missed! |
| | |
| *Nought.* | I should have done better, had I wist.* |
| | |
| *Mischief.* | Take heed, sirs, it stond you on hand.* |
| | *Curia tenta generalis,** |
| | In a place there* good ale is, |
| | *Anno regni regitalis* |
| | *Edwardi nullateni,** |
| | On yestern day in Feverere,* the year passeth fully,* |
| | As Nought hath written—here is our Tully*— |
| | *Anno regni regis nulli.** |

---

**fist:** Handwriting.

**wist:** Known.

**it stond you on hand:** It concerns you or is to your advantage.

***Curia tenta generalis:*** A Latin phrase, meaning, approximately, "The general court having taken place;" the full phrase more commonly used was "Curia generalis tenta ibidem." (Schlauch 1987). Both Manly (1897) and Furnivall and Pollard (1904) read "Carici" or "Carici" for "Curia"; however, this is more likely due to a copyist's sloppy "a" than to weak Latin. This passage and the following are examples of the types of Latin used in medieval English courtrooms and legal books.

**there:** Where.

***Anno regni regitalis / Edwardi nullateni:*** In the year of the reign of Edward the Nothingth. The manuscript is unclear here and may read "millateni," but "nullateni" seems more likley. Smart (1916) relies on this passage and the last line of this speech to date the play to the time Edward IV of England spent in exile during 1470 and 1471 at the end of the Wars of the Roses, during which time Edward and Henry VI were contesting the throne.

**yestern day in Feverere:** Literally, yesterday in February; here, it seems to refer to the last day in February, or possibly to be used as a nonsense date or referring to a general past time.

**the year passeth fully:** The year having come to an end. In fifteenth-century England, the year was sometimes considered to start on March 1.

**Tully:** May be a reference to Marcus Tullius Cicero, sometimes called Tully, a famous orator and lawyer to whom Nought is here being compared.

***Anno regni regis nulli:*** In the year of the reign of nobody.

56

*Nowadays.*　　What how, New Guise, thou makest much tarrying;*
　　　　　　That jacket shall not be worth a farthing.

　　　　　*Enter* NEW GUISE, *with a new, smaller jacket.*

*New Guise.*　Out of my way, sirs, for dread of* fighting!
　　　　　　Lo, here is a fit taille, light to leap about!*

*Nought.*　　It is not shapen* worth a morsel of bread—
　　　　　　There is too much cloth, it weighs as any* lead;
　　　　　　I shall go and mend it, else I will lose my head.
　　　　　　Make space, sirs, let me go out!

　　　　　*Exit* NOUGHT *with the jacket.*

*Mischief.*　Mankind, come hither. God send you the gout!*
　　　　　　Ye shall go to all the good fellows in the country about,
　　　　　　Unto the goodwife when the goodman is out.
　　　　　　"I will," say ye!

*Mankind.*　I will, sir.

---

**tarrying:** Delay. This word does not appear in the manuscript at all; it was added by Manly (1897), apparently to fill out the rhyme and meter, and has been followed by most later editors.

**for dread of:** Literally, out of fear of; here, to avoid.

**a fit taille, light to leap about:** A suitable cut of cloth for leaping about lightly.

**shapen:** Made; tailored.

**as any:** As much as any.

**gout:** It is not clear why Mischief wishes gout on Mankind here, except for the sake of the rhyme.

*New Guise.* There are but six deadly sins; lechery is none,
As it may be verified by us bretheles* everychon.*
Ye shall go rob, steal, and kill, as fast as you may goen.*
"I will," say ye!

*Mankind.* I will, sir.

*Nowadays.* On Sundays, on the morrow,* early betime,*
Ye shall with us to the ale-house early, to go dine,
And forbear mass and matins, hours and prime.*
"I will," say ye!

*Mankind.* I will, sir.

*Mischief.* Ye must have by your side a long *da pacem*,*
As true* men ride by the way, for to unbrace* them;
Take their money, cut their throats: thus overface* them.
"I will," say ye!

*Mankind.* I will, sir.

---

**bretheles:** It is possible the intended reading is "brethels," wretches, or "bretheles," breathless, or possibly a pun on both senses.

**everychon:** Every one; one and all; each one.

**goen:** Go.

**on the morrow:** In the morning.

**early betime:** Early in the morning; promptly.

**mass and matins, hours and prime:** Liturgical hours, at which devotions or prayers were said.

***da pacem:*** Sword; literally, in Latin, "give them peace."

**true:** Law-abiding.

**unbrace:** Literally the term means either to unfasten or release someone or something, or to carve or cut up a duck. The latter, specialized usage seems to fit most closely here.

**overface:** Overcome.

*Enter* NOUGHT.

*Nought.* Here is a jolly* jacket! How say ye?

*New Guise.* It is a good jake of fence* for a man's body.
Hey, dog! Hey, whoop, whoo! Go your way lightly;
Ye are well made for to run.

*Mischief.* Tidings! tidings! I have a-sped on!
Hence with your stuff! Fast we were gone!
I beshrew* the last shall come to his home.

*All.* Amen!

*Enter* MERCY.

*Mercy.* What ho, Mankind? Flee that fellowship, I you pray.

*Mankind.* I shall speak with thee another time; to-morn,* or the next day;
We shall go forth together to keep* my father's year-day.*
A tapster,* a tapster! Stow, statt, stow.*

---

**jolly:** Attractive; elegant.

**jake of fence:** Bruster and Rasmussen (2009) suggest that this is short for "jacket of defense," or a protective jacket.

**beshrew:** Curse; damn.

**to-morn:** Tomorrow.

**keep:** Observe; celebrate.

**year-day:** An anniversary; especially the anniversary of a person's death.

**tapster:** Bartender; tavern-keeper.

**Stow, statt, stow:** "Stow" was a call used to direct hunting hounds or call a hawk back to a falconer. For the middle word, Manly (1897) gives "stall," and Furnivall and Pollard (1904) "statt". The meaning is obscure; it might refer to the "stall" or decoy used by pickpockets to distract their victims.

*Mischief.*     A mischief go with; here I have a foul fall.
         Hence away from me, or I shall be-shit you all.

*New Guise.*  What ho, ostler, hostler,[+] lend us a football!
         Whoop, wow, a-now, a-now, a-now!

                    *Exit all but* MERCY.

---

**ostler, hostler:** So in the manuscript, although the words are usually used
     interchangeably to indicate an inkeeper or a keeper of horses.

# Scene 11

MERCY *alone.*

Mercy.  My mind is dispersed,* my body trembleth as the aspen leaf;
        The tears should trickle down by my cheeks, were not your
            reverence;*
        It were to me solace, the cruel visitation of death.
        Without rude behaviour I can* express this inconvenience;*
        Weeping, sighing, and sobbing were my sufficience.*
        All natural nutriment* to me as caren is odible;*
        My inward affliction yieldeth me* tedious unto your presence;
        I cannot bear it evenly, that Mankind is so flexible.

        Man unkind, wherever thou be! For all this world was not
            apprehensible*
        To discharge thine original offence, thraldom and capture,
        Till God's own well-beloved son was obedient and passable;*
        Every drop of his blood was shed to purge thine iniquity.

---

**dispersed:** Scattered.

**were not your reverence:** Were it not that you [God] inspire respect or
    veneration.

**can:** Manly (1897), followed by many later editors, considers this an error and
    that it should read "cannot."

**inconvenience:** Danger; sin; vice.

**were my sufficience:** Are (or would be) enough for me.

**nutriment:** Nourishment.

**as caren is odible:** Is as odious as carrion.

**yieldeth me:** Makes me; causes me to be.

**apprehensible:** Capable.

**passable:** Literally, capable of passing through. The exact sense intended here
    is not clear, but from context, it likely means something like "tractable."

I discommend and disallow* this often immutability.*
To every creature thou art despitous and odible;*
Why art thou so uncourteous, so inconsiderate? Alas, woe is
me!
As the fane* that turneth with the wind, so thou art
convertible.*

In trust is treason; this* promise is not credible;
This perversiose* ingratitude I cannot rehearse,*
To God and to all* the holy court of heaven, thou art
despicable,
As a noble versifier maketh mention in this verse:
*"Lex et natura, Christus et omnia iura*
*Damnant ingratum; lugetur eum fore natum."**
O good lady and mother of mercy, have pity and compassion
Of the wretchedness of Mankind, that is so wanton* and so
frail!*

---

**discommend and disallow:** Censure and refuse to praise.

**often immutability:** Frequent inconstancy.

**despitous and odible:** Spiteful and hateful.

**fane:** Weather vane; pennant or streamer.

**convertible:** Changeable.

**this:** So in the ms. Manly (1897) suggests "thy" for the manuscript's "this"
here and in the next line; he has been followed by many later editors.

**perversiose:** Wicked.

**rehearse:** Tell; relate.

**To God and to all:** Manly (1897) gives this unclear passage in the manuscript
as "To go over all;" Furnivall and Pollard (1904) have "To go over to
all." Most modern editions prefer the reading given here.

***"Lex et natura...":*** Law and nature, Christ and justice, lament the ungrateful
and grieve that he was born.

**wanton:** Reckless; rebellious; inappropriate.

**frail:** Morally weak; prone to sin.

Let mercy exceed justice, dear mother; admit this supplication:
Equity to be laid onparty,* and mercy to prevail.
Too sensual living is reprovable,* that is nowadays,
As by the comprehence* of this matter it may be specified:*
New Guise, Nowadays, Nought, with their allectuose* ways,
They have perverted Mankind, my sweet son, I have well
    espied.
Ah! With these cursed caitiffs,* an I may, he shall not long
    endure.
I, mercy, his father ghostly,* will proceed forth and do my
    property.*

Lady, help! This manner of living is a detestable pleasure;
*Vanitas vanitatum,** all is but vanity!
Mercy shall never be convicted of his uncourteous condition:
With weeping tears, by night and day, I will go, and never
    cease.
Shall I not find him? Yes, I hope. Now God be my protection!
My predilecte* son, where be ye? Mankind, *ubi es?**

*Exit* MERCY.

---

**laid onparty:** Set aside. Manly (1897) and Furnivall and Pollard (1904) both
    give the reading "laid over party."

**reprovable:** Blameworthy; reprehensible.

**comprehence:** Meaning; understanding.

**specified:** Made clear.

**allectuose:** Alluring.

**caitiffs:** Wretches.

**ghostly:** Spiritual; "ghostly father" may also refer to a priest, especially a
    confessor.

**do my property:** This use of "property" seems to be otherwise unattested, but
    the sense is probably to act in accordance with one's nature.

***Vanitas vanitatum*:** Vanity of vanities; a quotation from the Bible, Ecclesiastes
    1:2.

**predilecte:** Beloved; favored.

***ubi es?:*** Where are you?

# Scene 12

*Enter* MISCHIEF, NEW GUISE, NOWADAYS, *and* NOUGHT.

*Mischief.* My prepotent⁺ father, when ye sup, sup out your mess.⁺
Ye are all too-gloried⁺ in your terms; ye make many a lesse.⁺
Will ye hear? He crieth over Mankind *"ubi es?"*

*New Guise.* *Hic, hic, hic, hic, hic, hic, hic, hic!*⁺
That is to say, here, here, here, near dead in the creek!
If ye will have him, go and seek, seek, seek!
Seek not overlong, for losing of your mind!

*Nowadays.* If ye will have Mankind, how, *domine, domine, domine!*⁺
Ye must speak to the sheriff for a *cepi corpus.*⁺
Else ye must be fain⁺ to return with *non est inventus.*⁺
How say ye, sir? My bolt is shot.⁺

---

**prepotent:** Excellent.

**sup out your mess:** Finish your meal.

**too-gloried:** Overly boastful or proud.

**lesse:** Lie; some editors suggest this should be "lease."

***Hic, hic, hic...:*** Latin for "here," as explained in the following line. In the manuscript, there is no punctuation, and the second "hic" appears to be written as "hyc."

***domine:*** Master; a term of respect, especially for a clergyman.

**speak to the sheriff for a *cepi corpus*:** A *cepi corpus* is a legal writ for the arrest of a person, often for debt. Literally, it means "I have the body."

**fain:** Satisfied; content.

***non est inventus:*** Literally, "he is not found." This would be the sheriff's response to a writ where the debtor or defendant was not within his jurisdiction.

**My bolt is shot:** I have said my piece. A "bolt" is a type of missile, such as the short, heavy arrow shot from a crossbow; hence Nought's comical misunderstanding in the next line.

*Nought.*   I am doing of my needings;* beware how ye shot!
            Fie, fie, fie, I have foul arrayed* my foot!
            Be wise* for shooting with your tackles,* for, God wot,*
            My foot is foully overshot.*

*Mischief.*  A parliament, a parliament!* Come forth, Nought, behind!
            A counsel, belive!* I am afeared Mercy will him find.
            How say ye? And what say ye? How shall we do with
                Mankind?

*New Guise.* Tish, a fly's wing! Will ye do well?
            He weeneth* Mercy were hung for stealing of a mare;
            Mischief, go say to him that Mercy seeketh everywhere.
            He will hang himself, I undertake,* for fear.

*Mischief.*  I assent thereto; it is wittily said and well.

---

**doing of my needings:** Doing what is necessary; here, a euphemism for urinating or defecating.

**foul arrayed:** Foully or filthily adorned. Here, the context suggests that Nought has urinated on his own foot.

**wise:** Prudent; careful.

**tackles:** A pun; the word can refer to an archer's equipment or to a man's genitals.

**God wot:** God knows.

**overshot:** Another pun; the word can mean either an arrow that has flown past the target, or covered in excrement.

**parliament:** Conference; formal meeting.

**belive:** Quickly.

**weeneth:** Believes.

**undertake:** Assert.

| | |
|---|---|
| *Nowadays.* | Aye; whip* it in thy coat, anon* it were done.<br>Now St. Gabriel's mother* save the clouts of thy shoon!*<br>All the books in the world, if they had been undone,*<br>Could not a' counselled us bet.* |

MISCHIEF *goes offstage\* and returns with* MANKIND.

| | |
|---|---|
| *Mischief.* | How, Mankind! Come and speak with Mercy! He is here fast by.* |
| *Mankind.* | A rope, a rope, a rope! I am not worthy! |
| *Mischief.* | Anon, anon, anon! I have it here ready,<br>With a tree also that I have get.<br>Hold the tree, Nowadays; Nought, take heed and be wise! |
| *New Guise.* | Lo, Mankind, do as I do; this is the new guise.*<br>Give* the rope just to thy neck; this is mine advice. |

---

**whip:** Thrust; hide. Bruster and Rasmussen (2009) suggest that this refers to the rope Mischief will shortly produce for Mankind to hang himself with.

**anon:** Immediately.

**St. Gabriel's mother:** The reference is obscure and possibly nonsensical. The "St. Gabriel" referred to is probably the archangel.

**clouts of thy shoon:** The hobnails in your shoes.

**undone:** Opened.

**bet:** Better.

***Mischief goes offstage:*** One of the manuscript's few stage directions appears here: "Hic exit Myscheff," here exits Mischief. As he addresses Mankind in the next line, it is implied that he returns quickly with Mankind.

**fast by:** Nearby; close.

**new guise:** Latest fashion.

**Give:** The sense intended is unclear. This word ("gyff" in the manuscript) may also be intended for "gyve," to shackle.

*Enter* MERCY, *who threatens the vices with a rod or switch.*

*Mischief.*    Help thyself, Nought. Lo, Mercy is here!
              He scareth us with a baleis;* we may no longer tarry.

*New Guise.*  Quack, quack, quack! Alas, my throat! I beshrew* you, marry!*
              Ah, Mercy! Christ's copped* curse go with you, and Saint
                  Davy!
              Alas, my weasand!* Ye were somewhat too near!

*Exit* MISCHIEF, NOWADAYS, NEW GUISE, *and* NOUGHT.

---

**baleis:** Rod or switch used for flogging.

**beshrew:** Curse.

**marry:** Indeed.

**copped:** Utmost.

**weasand:** Windpipe.

# Scene 13

*Mercy.*      Arise, my precious, redempt* son! Ye be to me full dear.
         He is so timorous; me seemeth his vital spirit doth expire.

*Mankind.*    Alas! I have been so bestially disposed,* I dare not appear.
         To see your solacious* face I am not worthy to desire.

*Mercy.*      Your criminous* complaint woundeth my heart as a lance.
         Dispose yourself meekly to ask mercy, and I will assent.
         Yield me neither gold nor treasure, but your humble obesiance,
         The voluntary subjection of your heart, and I am content.

*Mankind.*    What, ask mercy yet once again? Alas, it were a wild* petition.
         Ever to offend, and ever to ask mercy: that is a puerility.*
         It is so abominable to rehearse* my wicked transgression!
         I am not worthy to have mercy, by no possibility.

*Mercy.*      O Mankind, my singler *solus*,* this is a lamentable excuse.
         The dolorous fears of my heart, how they begin to amount!*

---

**redempt:** Redeemed; restored.

**disposed:** Behaved.

**solacious:** Comforting, in a spiritual sense; consoling.

**criminous:** Guilty; recriminatory.

**wild:** Sinful; rash; reckless.

**puerility:** Immaturity; act of childishness.

**rehearse:** Describe; explain.

**singler *solus*:** Both words mean singular or unique, the first in English, the second in Latin. The sense seems to be a unique or exceptional individual.

**amount:** Increase; accumulate.

O blessed Jesu, help thou this sinful sinner to reduce:*
*Nam haec est mutatio dexterae Excelsi,* vertit impios et non sunt.*
Arise and ask mercy, Mankind, and be associate* to me;
Thy death shall be my heaviness.* Alas, tis pity it should be
    thus!
Thy obstinacy will exclude from* the glorious perpetuity.
Yet, for my love, ope* thy lips and say *"miserere mei, Deus!"**

Mankind.    The egal* justice of God will not permit such a sinful wretch
    To be revived and restored again; it were impossible.

Mercy.    The justice of God will, as I will, as himself doth preach:*
    *Nolo mortem peccatoris, inquit,** and if he will be reducible.*

---

**reduce:** Return or be restored to God. Furnivall and Pollard (1904) suggest
"redeem" instead.

***Nam haec est mutatio dexterae Excelsi:*** For this is the change of the right
hand of the Most High. A paraphrase of Psalm 77.

***vertit impios et non sunt:*** The wicked shall be overthrown and be no more. A
paraphrase of Proverbs 12:7.

**assoiciate:** Allied; joined.

**heaviness:** Sorrow.

**exclude from:** Bar you from.

**ope:** Open.

***miserere mei, Deus:*** Have mercy on me, God. This is from Psalm 51; it is the
same "neck verse" the vices memorized earlier in the play.

**egal:** Impartial; just.

**preach:** The manuscript reads "precyse."

***Nolo mortem peccatoris, inquit:*** I do not desire the death of sinners, he says.
A paraphrase of Ezekiel 33:11, used as a refrain in a popular poem of the
day, best known today in a sixteenth-century setting by composer
Thomas Morley.

**if he will be reducible:** If he is capable of being redeemed.

| | |
|---|---|
| *Mankind.* | Than* mercy, good mercy!<br>Little is our part of paradise, where mercy ne were.*<br>Good Mercy, excuse the inevitable objection of my ghostly*<br>    enemy;<br>The proverb sayeth: "The truth tryeth the self." Alas, I have<br>    much care! |
| *Mercy.* | God will not make you privy unto his last judgment;<br>Justice and equity shall be fortified,* I will not deny.<br>Truth may not so cruelly* proceed<br>But that Mercy shall rule* the matter without controversy.<br>Arise now, and go with me in this deambulatory.*<br>Incline your capacity;* my doctrine is convenient.*<br>Sin not in hope of mercy; that is a crime notorie.*<br>To trust overmuch in a prince, it is not expedient;<br>In hope, when ye sin, ye think to have mercy: beware of that<br>    adventure!* |

---

**Than:** Likely a pronoun. Alternatively, as this portion of the manuscript is more irregular, some variant of "Thanks" may be intended.

**where mercy ne were:** Were it not for mercy; if mercy were not there.

**ghostly:** Spiritual.

**fortified:** Upheld; made certain.

**cruelly:** Severely; mercilessly.

**rule:** Manage; control; decide.

**deambulatory:** Covered walkway; cloister.

**Incline your capacity:** The exact sense is unclear; most likely, Mercy is telling Mankind to actively apply himself to his own salvation.

**convenient:** Appropriate; timely.

**notorie:** Notorious.

**adventure:** Chance; risk.

The good Lord said to the lecherous woman of Canane—*
the holy gospel is the authority, as we read in scripture—
"*Vade et iam amplius noli peccare.*"*
Christ preserved this sinful woman taken in avowtry;*
He said to her these words: "Go, and sin no more."
So, to you: Go, and sin no more. Beware of vain confidence of
    mercy;*
Offend not a prince on trust of* his favour, as I said before.
If ye feel yourself trapped in the snare of your ghostly* enemy,
Ask mercy anon;* beware of the continuance.*
While a wound is fresh, it is proved curable by surgery
That, if it proceed overlong, it is cause of great grievance.*

---

**the lecherous woman of Canane:** The story of Jesus meeting the woman
taken in adultery is told in the Christian bible at John 8:1-11. Jesus tells
her accusers, who want to stone her to death, that the one among them
who has never sinned should throw the first stone. When her accusers
have left, Jesus tells the woman to go and sin no more.

In John, this event takes place near the Mount of Olives, in Jerusalem.
Canane (Chanane in the manuscript) is a Middle English name for what
is now more commonly called Canaan. The play is most likely conflating
the story of the woman taken in adultery with the unrelated story of the
exorcism of the Canaanite woman's daughter during a visit by Jesus to
Tyre and Sidon, as told in Matthew 15:21-28.

***Vade et iam amplius noli peccare:*** As translated by Mercy in the next few
lines, this is the Latin Vulgate version of Jesus' command, in John 8:11,
to the woman taken in adultery: "Go, and sin no more."

**avowtry:** Adultery.

**vain confidence of mercy:** In other words, Mercy is telling Mankind not to
rely on God's mercy to let him lead a sinful life and repent later.

**on trust of:** relying on.

**ghostly:** Spiritual.

**anon:** Soon; immediately.

**continuance:** Adjournment; delay.

**grievance:** Pain; injury.

*Mankind.*      To ask mercy and to have, this is a liberal* possession.

Shall this expeditious* petition ever* be allowed, as ye have insight?*

*Mercy.*      In this present life, mercy is plenty,* till death maketh his division,

But when ye be go,* *usque ad minimum quadrantem,** ye shall reckon this right.

Ask mercy and have, while the body with the soul hath his annexion;*

If ye tarry till your decease, ye may hap of your desire to miss.

Be repentant here, trust not the hour of death. Think on this lesson:

*Ecce nunc tempus acceptabile, ecce nunc dies salutis.**

All the virtue in the world, if ye might comprehend,

Your merits were not premiable* to the bliss above.

Not to the highest* joy of heaven, of your own proper effort to ascend:

With mercy ye may; I tell you no fable, scripture doth prove.

---

**liberal:** Generous; magnanimous.

**expeditious:** The meaning is unclear, but may be something like "quickly or easily granted."

**ever:** Always.

**as ye have insight:** To the extent that you know.

**plenty:** Plentiful; abundant.

**be go:** Are gone.

***usque ad minimum quadrantem:*** To the last farthing.

**annexion:** Connection; association.

***Ecce nunc tempus acceptabile, ecce nunc dies salutis:*** Behold, now is the accepted time; behold, now is the day of salvation. From the Christian bible, 2 Corinthians 6:2.

**premiable:** Deserving of the reward [of].

**highest:** This word is unclear in the manuscript. Manly (1900) gives "holest" and suggest "lowliest" or "lest" (least) as a suggested reading. Furnivall (1904) follows Manly, as do many modern editors. The manuscript seems closest to "hyest" or "holest."

| | |
|---|---|
| *Mankind.* | O Mercy, my suavious* solace and singular recreatory,* |
| | My predilect special,* ye are worthy to have my love; |
| | For, without desert,* and menes supplicatory,* |
| | Ye be compassionate to my inexcusable reproof.* |
| | Ah! It swemeth my heart* to think how unwisely I have |
| | wrought!* |
| | Titivilly, that goeth invisibly, hung his net before my eye, |
| | And, by his fantastical visions seditiously sought, |
| | By New Guise, Nowadays, Nought, caused me to obey. |
| | |
| *Mercy.* | Mankind, ye were oblivious of my doctrine meritory.* |
| | I said before Titvilly would assay you a bront.* |
| | Beware from henceforth of his fables delusory; |
| | The proverb sayeth: *Jacula prefata minus ledunt.** |

---

**suavious:** Pleasing. Manly (1900) and Furnivall (1904) read this word as "suatius;" Manly suggests "solatius," perhaps meaning "solace" as per the Latin or "rejoicing." The reading given by Bruster and Rasmussen (2009) is "suavious," meaning pleasing or agreeable; this is more consistent with both the manuscript and the context.

**recreatory:** Source of comfort.

**predilect special:** Particular favorite.

**desert:** Worthiness.

**menes supplicatory:** The exact sense is unclear. Menes may refer to complaints or petitions, which seems the most likely reading, but the grammatical structure of the sentence suggests that something has been omitted.

**reproof:** Shame.

**swemeth my heart:** Makes my heart grieve.

**wrought:** Acted; behaved. The term may imply bad behaviour.

**meritory:** Meritorious.

**assay you a bront:** Attack you; make a charge at you.

***Jacula prefata minus ledunt:*** Familiar darts cause less pain. This is the Latin as transcribed by Furnivall (1904); the transcriptions (and corrections) of this passage vary widely.

Ye have three adversaries, he is master of them all;
That is to say, the devil, the world, the flesh; and the fell,*
The New Guise, Nowadays, and Nought, the world we may
    them call;
And properly Titivilly signifies the fiend of hell.
The flesh: that is the unclean concupiescence* of your body.
These be your three ghostly* enemies, in whom ye have put
    your confidence.
They brought you to Mischief, to conclude your temporal
    glory,
As it hath been showed this worshipful audience.
Remember how ready I was to help you; from such I was not
    dangerous.
Wherefore, good son, abstain from sin evermore after this.
Ye may both save and spill* your soul, that is so precious:
*Libere welle, libere nolle,** God may not deny, in wis.*
Beware of Tityvilly with his net, and of all his envious will,
Of your sinful delectation* that grieveth your ghostly
    substance.*
Your body is your enemy; let him not have his will.
Take your leave when ye will; God send you good
    perseverance!*

---

**the fell:** The wicked ones. Manly (1900) suggests this should read "I thee tell."

**concupiescence:** Carnal desires; lust.

**ghostly:** Spiritual.

**spill:** Damn.

***Libere welle, libere nolle:*** There is some debate over the precise meaning of this latin tag, but the sense is that man has free will and can choose to exercise it to act either well or badly. Both Manly (1900) and Furnivall (1904) mistranscribe this as "Libere welle, libere welle."

**in wis:** Indeed; certainly.

**delectation:** Sensual pleasure.

**grieveth your ghostly substance:** Injures your soul.

**good perseverance:** Long life; continued righteousness.

74

*Mankind.*   Sith* I shall depart, bless me, father, ere than* I go.
            God send us all plenty of his great mercy!

*Mercy.*     *Dominus custodiat te ab omni malo,*
            *In nomine patris, et filii, et spiritus sancti.** Amen!

*Exit* MANKIND.

---

**sith:** Since.

**ere than:** Before. Both Manly (1900) and Furnivall (1904) give this as "here then," which does appear consistent with the manuscript, but makes less sense in context.

***Dominus custodiat te...:*** God preserve you from all evil, in the name of the Father, the Son, and the Holy Spirit.

# Epilogue

*Mercy.*  Worshipful sovereigns! I have do my property\*:
Mankind is delivered by my favorable\* patrocinie.\*
God preserve him from all wicked captivity,
And send him grace his sensual condition\* to mortify.
Now for his love, that for us received his humanity,
Search your conditions\* with due examination!
Think, and remember: the world is but a vanity,\*
As is proved daily by diverse mutation.\*
Mankind is wretched, he hath sufficient proof;
Therefore, God keep\* you all *per suam misericordiam,*\*
That ye may be pleasurous\* with the angels above,
And have to your portion\* *vitam eternam.*\* Amen!

---

**I have do my property:** The literal meaning is obscure, but the sense is clearly "my job is done."

**favorable:** There is significant disagreement over the proper reading of this word. Manly (1900) gives it as "sunerall"; Furnivall (1904) as "suuerall"; Farmer (1909) as "several." Most modern editors read the initial letter as an f rather than a long s, with Bruster and Rasmussen (2009) reading it as "favoural" and Fitzgerald and Sebastian (2012) as "faverall."

**patrocinie:** Protection. This seems to be the only known use of this word in Middle or Early Modern English, and is likely another of Mercy's newly coined Latinisms.

**sensual condition:** Carnal nature, habits, or behvior.

**conditions:** Character; habits; characteristics.

**a vanity:** Worthless; a thing of no value.

**diverse mutation:** Various changes.

**keep:** No such word appears in the manuscript, but editors have uniformly agreed that one must have been omitted. Manly (1900) and Furnivall (1904) suggest "keep;" most modern editors prefer "grant."

***per suam misericordiam:*** In his mercy.

**pleasurous:** Happy; joyous.

**to your portion:** As your share; as your inheritance.

***vitam eternam:*** Eternal life.

# Appendix

These appendices contain additional materials related to the play and its subject matter. First, there is an extract from Joseph Quincy Adams' *Shakespearean Playhouses,* in which Adams uses *Mankind* as an example of how plays would have been performed in the days before there were regular theaters in London. This is followed by selections from the original introduction to F. J. Furnivall's 1904 edition of *Mankind.*

# Mankind in the Inn-Yards

*This is a lightly edited extract from the first chapter of* Shakespearean Playhouses: A History of English Theatres from the Beginnings to the Restoration, *Joseph Quincy Adams, Jr.'s 1917 book-length study of early London theaters. In this chapter, "The Inn-Yards," Adams, a Shakespeare scholar and the first director of the Folger Shakespeare Library, uses* Mankind *as an example of the way plays were presented in the days before there were regular playhouses in London.*

Before the building of regular playhouses the itinerant troupes of actors were accustomed, except when received into private homes, to give their performances in any place that chance provided, such as open street-squares, barns, town-halls, moot-courts, schoolhouses, churches, and—most frequently of all, perhaps—the yards of inns. These yards, especially those of carriers' inns, were admirably suited to dramatic representations, consisting as they did of a large open court surrounded by two or more galleries. Many examples of such inn-yards are still to be seen in various parts of England.

In the yard a temporary platform—a few boards, it may be, set on barrel-heads—could be erected for a stage; in the adjacent stables a dressing-room could be provided for the actors; the rabble—always the larger and more enthusiastic part of the audience—could be accommodated with standing-room about the stage; while the more aristocratic members of the audience could be comfortably seated in the galleries overhead. Thus a ready-made and very serviceable theatre was always at the command of the players; and it seems to have been frequently made use of from the very beginning of professionalism in acting.

One of the earliest extant moralities, *Mankind,* acted by strollers in the latter half of the fifteenth century, gives us an interesting glimpse of an inn-yard performance. The opening speech makes distinct reference to the two classes of the audience described above as occupying the galleries and the yard:

> O ye sovereigns that sit, and ye brothers that stand right up.

The "brothers," indeed, seem to have stood up so closely about the stage that the actors had great difficulty in passing to and from their dressing-room. Thus, Nowadays leaves the stage with the request:

> Make space, sirs, let me go out!

New Gyse enters with the threat:

> Out of my way, sirs, for dread of a beating!
> Make space, sirs, let me go out!

While Nought, with even less respect, shouts:

> Avaunt, knaves! Let me go by!

Language such as this would hardly be appropriate if addressed to the "sovereigns" who sat in the galleries above; but, as addressed to the "brothers," it probably served to create a general feeling of good nature. And a feeling of good nature was desirable, for the actors were facing the difficult problem of inducing the audience to pay for its entertainment.

This problem they met by taking advantage of the most thrilling moment of the plot. The Vice and his wicked though jolly companions, having wholly failed to overcome the hero, Mankind, decide to call to their assistance no less a person than the great Devil himself; and accordingly they summon him with a "Walsingham wystyle." Immediately he roars in the dressing-room, and shouts:

> I come, with my legs under me!

There is a flash of powder, and an explosion of fireworks, while the eager spectators crane their necks to view the entrance of this "abhomynabull" personage. But nothing appears; and in the expectant silence that follows the actors calmly announce a collection of money, facetiously making the appearance of the Devil dependent on the liberality of the audience:

*New Gyse.* Now ghostly to our purpose, worshipful sovereigns,
We intend to gather money, if it please your negligence.
For a man with a head that of great omnipotence—

*Nowadays (interrupting).* Keep your tale, in goodness, I pray you, good
              brother!

*[Addressing the audience, and pointing towards the dressing-room, where the Devil
roars again.]*

    He is a worshipful man, sirs, saving your reverence.
    He loveth no groats, nor pence, or two-pence;
    Give us red royals, if ye will see his abominable presence.

*New Gyse.*   Not so! Ye that may not pay the one, pay the other.

And with such phrases as "God bless you, master," "Ye will not
say nay," "Let us go by," "Do them all pay," "Well mote ye fare," they
pass through the audience gathering their groats, pence, and twopence;
after which they remount the stage, fetch in the Devil, and continue
their play without further interruption.

In the smaller towns the itinerant players might, through a letter of
recommendation from their noble patron, or through the good-will of
some local dignitary, secure the use of the town-hall, of the
schoolhouse, or even of the village church. In such buildings, of course,
they could give their performances more advantageously, for they could
place money-takers at the doors, and exact adequate payment from all
who entered. In the great city of London, however, the players were
necessarily forced to make use almost entirely of public inn-yards—an
arrangement which, we may well believe, they found far from
satisfactory. Not being masters of the inns, they were merely tolerated;
they had to content themselves with hastily provided and inadequate
stage facilities; and, worst of all, for their recompense they had to trust
to a hat collection, at best a poor means of securing money. Often too,
no doubt, they could not get the use of a given inn-yard when they
most needed it, as on holidays and festive occasions; and at all times
they had to leave the public in uncertainty as to where or when plays
were to be seen. Their street parade, with the noise of trumpets and
drums, might gather a motley crowd for the yard, but in so large a place
as London it was inadequate for advertisement among the better
classes. And as the troupes of the city increased in wealth and dignity,
and as the playgoing public grew in size and importance, the old
makeshift arrangement became more and more unsatisfactory.

At last the unsatisfactory situation was relieved by the specific dedication of certain large inns to dramatic purposes; that is, the proprietors of certain inns found it to their advantage to subordinate their ordinary business to the urgent demands of the actors and the playgoing public. Accordingly they erected in their yards permanent stages adequately equipped for dramatic representations, constructed in their galleries wooden benches to accommodate as many spectators as possible, and were ready to let the use of their buildings to the actors on an agreement by which the proprietor shared with the troupe in the "takings" at the door. Thus there came into existence a number of inn-playhouses, where the actors, as masters of the place, could make themselves quite at home, and where the public without special notification could be sure of always finding dramatic entertainment.

Richard Flecknoe, in his *Discourse of the English Stage* (1664), goes so far as to dignify these reconstructed inns with the name "theatres." At first, says he, the players acted "without any certain theatres or set companions, till about the beginning of Queen Elizabeth's reign they began here to assemble into companies, and set up theatres, first in the city (as in the inn-yards of the Cross Keys and Bull in Grace and Bishop's Gate Street at this day to be seen), till that fanatic spirit [i.e., Puritanism], which then began with the stage and after ended with the throne, banished them thence into the suburbs"—that is, into Shoreditch and the Bankside, where, outside the jurisdiction of the puritanical city fathers, they erected their first regular playhouses.

The "banishment" referred to by Flecknoe was the Order of the Common Council issued on December 6, 1574. This famous document described public acting as then taking place "in great inns, having chambers and secret places adjoining to their open stages and galleries"; and it ordered that henceforth "no inn-keeper, tavern-keeper, nor other person whatsoever within the liberties of this city shall openly show, or play, nor cause or suffer to be openly showed or played within the house yard or any other place within the liberties of this city, any play," etc.

How many inns were let on special occasions for dramatic purposes we cannot say; but there were five "great inns," more famous than the rest, which were regularly used by the best London troupes. Thus Howes, in his continuation of Stow's *Annals*, in attempting to give a list of the playhouses which had been erected "within London and the suburbs," begins with the statement, "Five inns, or common osteryes, turned to playhouses." These five were the Bell and the Cross Keys, hard by each other in Gracechurch Street, the Bull, in Bishopsgate Street, the Bell Savage, on Ludgate Hill, and the Boar's Head, in Whitechapel Street without Aldgate. (All historians of the drama have confused this great carriers' inn with the Boar's Head in Eastcheap made famous by Falstaff.)

In 1664, as Flecknoe tells us, the Cross Keys and the Bull still gave evidence of their former use as playhouses; perhaps even then they were occasionally let for fencing and other contests. In 1666 the great fire completely destroyed the Bell, the Cross Keys, and the Bell Savage; the Bull, however, escaped, and enjoyed a prosperous career for many years after. Samuel Pepys was numbered among its patrons, and writers of the Restoration make frequent reference to it. What became of the Boar's Head without Aldgate I am unable to learn; its memory, however, is perpetuated to-day in Boar's Head Yard, between Middlesex Street and Goulston Street, Whitechapel.

# Introduction to the 1904 Edition

*One of the source texts for this Groundling Press edition is the first complete printed text of the three Macro Plays, published in 1904 and edited by Frederick James Furnivall, who was one of the three founders of the Oxford English Dictionary, and Shakespeare scholar Alfred William Pollard. The following are some of Pollard's observations on the play from his Introduction.*

The three morality plays here printed by the kindness of their present owner, Mr. J. H. Gurney, of Keswick Hall, near Norwich, once formed part of the collection of the Rev. Cox Macro, whence the name, the Macro Moralities, by which they are usually quoted. According to a useful notice in the *Dictionary of National Biography,* Cox Macro was born in 1683, and was the son of Thomas Macro, a wealthy grocer of Bury St. Edmunds, who was five times Mayor of that town. Thomas Macro had bought an estate at Little Haugh, Norton, as a country residence, and here his son Cox lived and died, devoting himself to antiquarian pursuits, though be had qualified himself as a physician, and had also taken holy orders. He bought antiquities of many kinds, and in 1766 a catalogue of them was printed. According to the *Dictionary of National Biography,* "many of his manuscripts had belonged to Sir Henry Spelman, others formed part of the library of Bury Abbey." Cox Macro died in 1767, and fifty-two years later his manuscripts were in the possession of John Patteson, M.P. for Norwich, who unadvisedly sold them (it is said for no more than £150) to a bookseller of that town. The following year they were put up for auction at Christie's, and while forty-one lots were bought by Dawson Turner, the rest, including the Moralities, were bought for £700 by Mr. Hudson Gurney, in whose family they have since remained. About 1882, when Dr. Furnivall was editing the *Digby Plays* for the New Shakspere Society, he obtained leave for a copy of the *Macro Plays* to be made by Miss Eleanor Marx (daughter of Karl), and expressed the hope that he might edit it for the Society, "when we have any money to spare." The transcript was subsequently transferred to the Early English Text Society, and in 1890, when I was preparing my *English Miracle Plays, Moralities and Interludes* for the Clarendon Press, Dr. Furnivall permitted me to read it, and publish extracts from one of the plays, *The Castle of Perseverance.* In the introduction to my volume of selections I in my turn expressed the hope that I might edit the Macro Plays, and I was very kindly asked by Mr. Gurney to stay with him in order to study the manuscript. Illness in my family interfered with this arrangement, and then I went off to Chaucer and bibliography till I had my hands full, and the E.E.T.S., which has always (see its prospectuses) copy which will cost £2000 to print ready to be sent to press at short notice, seemed quite content to leave me alone.

In the present summer, however, Dr. Furnivall began to fulfil his promise by editing the text and called on me to fulfil mine by writing this Introduction. Of course, as he always does when be means to have it, he got his own way, but the summons came at a very inconvenient time, and I hope that this may be taken as an excuse for my not having gone more deeply into the local and political allusions, which are worth much more careful research than I have been able to give to them, though it is not by any means certain that the research would be rewarded by substantial discoveries. I should like to add to this history of the present edition that Dr. Furnivall, who, when I get him as a visitor to meetings of the Bibliographical Society, is fond of calling me a Duke (because he envies our finances), has certainly treated me like one, in taking to himself all the hard work of preparing the text for press, and leaving me to come in, as a commentator and critic, with a nice printed text to work upon.

### Mankind

Of the three plays here printed, that which has been bound up first in the manuscript is undoubtedly the latest. The handling of its subject shows us that in *Mankind* the morality play is approaching its sixteenth-century degradation, while the Latinisms which abound in the speeches intended to be dignified also make for a late date. By his use in l. 683 of Edward as an obvious name for a king, the playwright himself suggests to us that he wrote when Edward IV had been for some time firmly seated on his throne, and 1475, the end of the third quarter of the fifteenth century, seems as good a round date for the composition of the play as we can take. As regards the district in and for which the author wrote there is still more abundant evidence. The dialect is that of the Eastern Counties, and the local references are numerous. Besides an oath by St. Anne (l. 75), whose increasing importance during the fifteenth century was, I think, especially noticeable in the Eastern Counties, we have (l. 621) another by St. Audray, *i.e.* St. Etheldreda, whose shrine was one of the chief glories of Ely Cathedral, and who in our next play (l. 936) is expressly called "Sent Audre of Ely." In l. 266 wc hear of a "tapster of Bury"; in l. 445 of "a Walsyngham wystull"; finally in ll. 498-508 we come on allusions to a number of private persons living in the neighbourhoods of Cambridge and of King's Lynn in Norfolk. The names of the first two places mentioned (ll. 498, 499) are read by Dr. Furnivall as Sanston and Hanston, for which he proposes doubtfully Santon on the borders of Suffolk and Norfolk, and either Ampton in Suffolk or Hunston, *i.e.* Hunstanton, in Norfolk. Dr. Brondl at the suggestion of Dr. W. Stevenson reads "Sauston" and "hauston," and identifies the towns with Sawston and Hauxton, both near Cambridge.

If this be right, and we add to them Trumpington (l. 500), we begin with three places in the Cambridge district, to which follow Walton (l. 502) and Gayton (l. 503), each about eight miles to the east of King's Lynn and only three or four miles apart. The remaining four places are alternated, Fulbourn (l. 554) being some five miles E.S.E. of Cambridge; Massingham (l. 506) in Norfolk, some five miles from Gayton, and about twelve from Lynn; Bottisham (Botysam, l. 507), some seven miles E.N.E. of Cambridge; Swaffham (Soffeham, l. 508) in Norfolk, about the same distance from Walton, and about fourteen from Lynn. This arrangement of three Cambridge places, two Norfolk, a Cambridge, a Norfolk, a Cambridge, a Norfolk, can hardly be accidental. It has much more the appearance of a deliberate attempt to keep up interest in two different districts by local allusions very equitably distributed. Now in ll. 448-467, before the principal devil Titivillus is suffered to enter, the players tell the spectators roundly that they are going to gather money, "Ellys ther xall no man hym se." They then call on the audience in a truly delightful phrase: "Gyf ws rede royallys, yf ye wyll se hys abhomynabull presens," though another speaker, mindful that not every one would carry red royals about him, thoughtfully makes a correction to admit of minor offerings of groats, pennies and twopences, by calling out "Not so! ye that mow not pay the ton, pay the tother." The collection, thus freely spoken of as a payment, is to begin at "the goode man of this house," and it is thus clear that we are dealing with a company of players giving their performance very definitely for gain, in or before a house. The two sets of places to which the players allude forbid us to localize the play either at the town of Cambridge or at that of King's Lynn, for a town audience would have taken no interest in these references to village worthies. We must therefore regard the players as strollers, touring in two neighbouring districts, and almost certainly acting in the courtyards of inns, since in l. 725, when New-Guise wants a football, he calls to an ostler to lend him one.

The fact that the play was written for such a company as this, acting not for the honour of the guild to which they belonged, nor for the pleasure and instruction of their own townsfolk, but with the object of gaining money from the less educated audiences of country districts gathered in inn-yards, sufficiently accounts for the low tone which runs through it.

In taking a general glance at the play the first thing we may note is that the forces of morality and immorality are very unevenly distributed. On the one side is Mercy single-handed, on the other Mischief with three subordinate combatants, Nought, New-Guise and Now-a-days. In the middle of the play Mischief yields the command of the forces of disorder to the devil of abominable presence already mentioned, Titivillus. Before Mischief leaves the stage to make room for him, the voice of Titivillus is heard outside, and only eighteen lines of verse intervene before his arrival. As, however, the collection was taking place during these, and there would probably be some exchange of chaff between the actors and audience, it is possible that Mischief had time to make a quick change, and that the chief actor doubled this part with that of Titivillus. In any case not more than seven players would be needed, and as there is no mention of any properties beyond a net for Titivillus, it is obvious that the strollers could arrive at a village with their stage-dresses in their wallets, and give their performance wherever they saw chance of profit. We must picture them to ourselves, however, not as sauntering to their destinations along green lanes, but rather as trudging through mire and snow, for several allusions point to the play having been written for performance at Christmas, or at least in the winter. Thus in l. 54 Mischief says that he has hired himself as a "Winter corn-thresher," and in l. 325 Now-a-days tells the audience "We wyll cum gyf yow a Crystemes songe." Just before this (l. 316) New-Guise has remarked, "The wether ys colde: Gode sende ws goode ferys," while in l. 725 he calls for a football. Moreover, at l. 539 Mankind, when he is digging his land, announces, "I xall sow my corn at wyntur, & lett Gode work"; and although from the preceding lines (he has been badly hampered by the plank which Titivillus has put in the way of his spade) this might mean, "I will put off sowing my corn until the winter," the fact that he immediately looks round for his seed, shows that this also is a reference to winter as the time of action.

The play begins with a speech by Mercy on the necessity of good works. The penultimate line, "The corn xall be sauyde, the chaff xall be brent," gives a cue to Mischief, who despite the chilly remark of Mercy, "Why come ye hethyr, brother? ye were not dysyryde," proceeds to demonstrate by the verse, "Corn seruit bredibus, chaffe horsibus, straw fyrybusque," that to burn chaff was to put it to a wrong use. Mercy can only reply with the charming couplet: "A-voyde, goode brother! ye ben culpable To interrupte thus my talkynge delectable," but Mischief refuses to go ("I am cumme hedyr to make yow game" is his plea), and it is possible that a gap which here occurs in the text may have been caused by some earlier copyist finding Mischief's conversation a little too unedifying. When we reach the other side of the gap we find that minstrels are playing, and that Nought, New-Guise and Now-a-days have entered, and are trying to make Mercy dance. Apparently (from l. 111) Mercy in a lost speech had attributed some of the evils of the times to new-fangled follies and fashions, and the young devils pretend that they have come on his invitation. He disclaims knowledge of them, and when they ask his name, having given their own, he answers loftily:

> "Mercy ys my name and my denomynacyon.
> I conseyve ye haue but a little faus in my communycacyon."

On this New-Guise comments justly but irreverently, "Ey, ey! yower body ys full of Englysch Laten," and proceeds to propound a ribald sentence, and bid Mercy "opyn yowur sachell with Laten wordis," and translate it in "clerycall manere." Mercy at last gets rid of his three "onthryfty gestis," and consoles himself with a short soliloquy, ending with the advice to the audience to take what is good in new fashions and leave the bad.

All that has taken place up to this point may be regarded as a kind of Prologue showing the rival forces, with one or other of which the hero will have to ally himself. Mankind now enters, and in the wonders of his "Englysch Laten" leaves Mercy altogether in the shade. Nevertheless, in his sorrow to find his soul "assocyat with my flesch, that stynkyng dunge-hyll," he goes to Mercy for ghostly solace. This

Mercy imparts, and (since the author now concentrates all his Latinisms on Mankind) in plainer English than he has yet used. The last stanza of his speech is quite in the vulgar tongue:

> "Yf a man haue an hors, and kepe hym not to hye,
> He may then reull hym at hys own dysyere:
> Yf he be fede ouer well, he wyll dysobey,
> And in happe cast his master in the myre."

Unluckily this homely simile attracts New-Guise and his fellows, who come in to make fun of it. But they only stay a minute, and Mercy has time to finish his warnings, which end rather prettily with the lines:

> "Yf ye disples Gode, aske Mercy a-non,
> Ellys Myscheff wyll be redy to brace yow in hys brydyll.
> Kysse me now, my dere darlynge! Gode schelde yow from
>     yower fon!
> Do truly yowur labure, and be nevere ydyll!
> The blyssynge of Gode be with yow & with all thes
>     worschypfull men."

Left to himself, Mankind indulges in some more Latinisms ("sacyatt," "mellyfluouse" and "superatt" are in the first four lines), and then betakes him to digging, though apparently, since he remarks "To eschew ydullnes, I do yt myn own selffe," with a distinct sense of condescension. Of course the devils are now down on him, singing what they call a "Crystemes songe" for which they ought to have been rolled in a midden, and chaffing him unmercifully, till he puts them to flight by vigorous blows of his spade. "I xall convycte them, I hope, everychon," is his triumphant comment; and in the fulness of hie heart he vows to "lyue euer with labure, to correct my insolence." Meanwhile he has to fetch some seed-corn, so he goes out, promising the spectators "ryght sone I xall reverte."

While Mankind is gone to fetch his seed, there is a little pause in the action, during which Mischief consoles his sweet babes for the blows they have received, and a collection is made among the spectators, the entrance of the superior devil Titivillus being made dependent on a satisfactory "gathering." As soon as he comes in, Titivillus asks New-Guise to lend him a penny. But the smaller devils all profess that their purses are empty and they are sent off on a foray, with advice as to some inhabitants of the Cambridgeshire and Norfolk villages already mentioned, as persons either to be sought out or avoided. Having dismissed his young friends with a left-handed blessing, Titivillus, in pursuance of his desire that "the goode man Mercy" shall no longer be Mankind's guide, hides a board in the ground to prevent the condescending digger from getting his spade in. While Mankind is struggling complainingly with this obstacle, the seed-corn is stolen, either by Titivillus or by some confederate boy in the audience (imagine that boy's delight!), and Mankind throws down his spade, and bidding farewell to labour, thinks he will hear his evensong (l. 544) by saying a Paternoster. Titivillus, however, who is supposed to be invisible, whispers to him "A schorte preyere thyrlyth hewyn," no doubt spoiling this fine phrase by a diabolical emphasis on the word "schorte." He adds force to this argument by a more physical suggestion, and Mankind explains to the audience that he "wyll go do that nedis must be done" in the yard. What alternative was open to him is not indicated, but Titivillus triumphs greatly, and plainly considers that if Mankind could only be killed at this moment his soul would be lost. When Mankind returns, the time for evensong is over, and out of patience with both labour and prayer, he goes to sleep. As he sleeps, Titivillus instils into him the belief that Mercy has been hanged, and that his only course is to make friends with New-Guise, Now-a-days and Nought. The smaller devils now return from adventures in which New-Guise has only been saved from hanging by the rope breaking, and are joined by Mischief. Mankind asks forgiveness for his performances with his spade, and Mischief decrees that he must make his submission in form of law. Proclamation is made to "all maner of men and comun women" and a manorial court is opened. The young devils, however, prefer to make their profit off Mankind by persuading him to give them his gown to be cut down into a fashionable short jacket, leaving them the superfluous cloth as a perquisite. Much to our loss, therefore, the parody of the proceedings in a manor-court is not carried further. Mankind and the young devils are now excellent friends, and after telling him that henceforth he must "forber masse and matens, owres and pryme" (Protestant controversialists, please mark that the obligation on holy days was not merely to hear mass), they are running off with him to play football (by courtesy of the ostler) when in comes Mercy, and bids Mankind "fle that felyschyppe." Fully hardened in his bad courses, the wretched Mankind puts off his monitor until another time, "to-morne or the next day," and goes off to play football on the obviously trumped-up excuse that it is his father's birthday (l. 721)!

Left on the stage by himself, Mercy has nothing to do but soliloquize, and the treacherous playwright treats him far from fairly. His grief, he is made to say, is so great that

> "Without rude behauer I kannot expresse this inconvenyens;
> Wepynge, sythynge & sobbinge were my suffycyens;
> All naturall nutriment, to me, as caren, ys odybull;
> My inwarde affiixcyon ʒeldyth me tedyouse unto yowur
>     presens;
> I kan not bere yt ewynly, that mankynde ys so flexibull."

So mourns Mercy for some forty lines, on purpose to provoke the comment of Mischief "ye are all to-gloryede in yowur termys." Nevertheless the determination of Mercy to seek out Mankind fills the devils with alarm, and they resolve to work on Mankind's sense of shame to make him hang himself. They almost succeed, but Mercy attacks them with a scourge, and they flee, leaving Mankind alone with Mercy. With many terribly long words on both sides Mankind is persuaded that he has not sinned beyond the possibility of pardon, and with a final address by Mercy to the "wyrschepfull sofereyns" in the audience the play comes to an end.

If it had not been for Dr. Furnivall's express orders I should have thought his side-notes a sufficient clue to the outlines of this play of *Mankind*, and have forborne to waste paper and print over an analysis. My obedience has been well repaid as far as my personal understanding of the play is concerned, for whether my estimate of it is right or wrong it is certainly definite. Judged by the original standard of the morality play, it is about as degraded a composition as can well be conceived, and is interesting precisely because it shows the theory, that moral teaching should be made pleasurable by giving it the form of a play, carried out to its inevitable end in caricature. For that this playwright, in his determination to please the inn-yard audience in return for their groats and pence, deliberately made fun of Mercy, there can be no doubt whatever. Medieval simplicity could go to great lengths of what seems to us hardy irreverence. When the angels have sung their "Glory to God in the Highest," the shepherds imitate them with cracked voices, and no doubt the spectators laughed and were meant to laugh. The tension was broken as the playwright wished it to be, but the

Gloria sung above the stage by the best voices that could be found remained unsullied. More striking still, when God is heard reproving Cain, Cain answers back with "Who is that hob-ouer-the wall?" and declares hardily "God is out of hys wit" (*Towneley Plays*, II, 300). Cain out of his own nature ridicules God, but the words assigned to God are not themselves ridiculous, and the spectators, though they may have laughed at the moment, knew, if so, that they were laughing on the wrong side. But in this play of *Mankind* the author deliberately gets fun out of Mercy, and of his hero also when his hero is in a moral mood, by making them talk an English Latin, which few of the audience could have understood, and then turns Mercy into ridicule for doing it. He takes the whole of the moralizing in the play as mere common form; and as people who moralize are apt to use long words, makes them use the longest he can find, so that the audience may have something to laugh at, even when the devils are off the stage. This, of course, was a breach of covenant, but it was the inevitable result of obliging playwrights and actors to preach, when their only desire was beginning to be to amuse. Heywood's *Johan Johan*, with its frank appreciation of the humours of cuckoldry, is a much more edifying performance than this moral play of *Mankind*, and the fact may be commended to those who think that English playwrights could ever have developed comedy and tragedy out of the medieval religious and moral drama without the aid of French, Latin and Italian new models to help them.

While I am leaving the philological commentary on these plays to be written by Dr. Furnivall, I may note from the very old-fashioned side from which I am interested in the history of words that the Latinisms in the speeches of Mercy and Mankind (in his moral moments) offer a rich harvest to the historical dictionaries. Any one who consults the Oxford Dictionary will see how speedily its editors fastened on Dr. Brandl's text published in 1898, and in the volumes of the Dictionary issued before that year we can bring back the dates of the first occurrence of some words by over a century and a half. Thus *annexion* (l. 850) is not registered in the Oxford Dictionary until 1610, *apprehensible* (l. 735) till 1635, *approximate* (l. 216) till 1646, *convict* (l. 398) in the sense of "vanquish" till 1595, *expeditious* (l. 853) till 1610. *Allectuous* (l. 754), *dalyacyon* (l. 46), *interleccyon* (l. 442) and *intermyse* (l. 290) are not in the Dictionary at all, I hope for what would be the best of all reasons, that no one save the author of this play ever used them. Others of our author's long words had already been introduced by Wyclif; in others he just anticipates Fabyan. There is of course no reason to suppose that Fabyan had read *Mankind*, or that the author of *Mankind* had read Wyclif, much less that the use of *annexion, apprehensible, approximate,* etc., in the seventeenth century was in any way influenced by this play. As long as Latin was the learned language of all Europe, any vernacular which had any capacity for admitting Latinisms had to suffer from these intrusions, which tried their luck again and again whenever they came readily to the pen of any author who could not think of an English word to express what he meant. On the whole, English has not done badly with them. It is only the poetry written between 1450 and 1550 with which they have played havoc, and the experiment as to whether they were or were not fitted to lend dignity to verse no doubt had to be tried. The sin of our author lay in the fact that he saw how unsuited they were to verse intended to appeal to simple folk, and amused himself by crowding them into his lines, and then making fun of them.

One side issue of the Latinizing extravagances in Mankind may be worth another paragraph. Our playwright was a miserably poor poet, as is attested by the badness of his rimes. Some deduction must be made for dialect influence, which may have helped him in riming *e* and *i* or *y*, *ey* and *y*, *o* and *a*. But his ear was clearly often satisfied with the rawest assonances, as in *speke* and *slepe* (st. 14), *hony* and *body*, *man* and *terram* (st. 34), *tyme* and *wyn* (st. 36), *faytaur, master, playster* (st. 39), *anon* and *hom* (st. 42), *mell, delffe, selffe* (st. 54), *wepyn,* i. e. weapon, *beten,* and *wepyn,* to weep (st. 65), *tyme, dyne, prime* (st. 102), *aspen leffe* and *deth* (st. 105). On the other hand his verses have less of the painful jog-trot of this period than those of many better poets, and some of his lines are rather good as prose, and anticipate the prose rhythms of the time when the place of the Latin element in English had been successfully settled. Thus in l. 110 the sarcasm of Mercy, "He was well occupyede that browte yow, brethern," is very neatly phrased; l. 180, "Take that ys to be takyn, & leue that ys to be refusyde," is excellently direct; l. 815, "Euer to offend & euer to aske mercy, that ys a puerilite," has a nice balance, and even l. 830, "Good Mercy, excuse the ineuytabyll obieccion of my gostly enemy," though it is bad enough, is amusingly modern.

The leaves of the manuscript of *Mankind* are numbered 122-134. The figures of this numeration of the leaves appear to be of the eighteenth century. At this stage of its career the collection contained three other manuscripts, a Juvenal on vellum, the laws of Ina and Aethelstan, and a treatise on Alchemy, in strange juxtaposition. The three moralities were separated from these other pieces shortly after the Macro sale in 1820, and are now bound in blue morocco stamped with the arms of Mr. Hudson Gurney. When this was done, *Mankind*, which in the earlier volume had followed *Mind, Will and Understanding*, as is shown by the numeration of the leaves, was placed in front of it, so that it now begins the volume.

Thirteen leaves of quarto paper, measuring 220 x 158 mms. Written throughout in the same hand, though the last four pages with a softer pen and different ink. Probable date of writing about 1475. The watermark of the paper is a glove or gauntlet and star, the lower part of the gauntlet being of an unusual shape, so that when seen on one side of the fold of paper, by which, as in all quarto books, the watermark is cut in half, it looks almost like the top of an ewer.

When collated by watermarks, the manuscript is seen to be made up of a gathering of twelve leaves preceded by the leaf now numbered 122, which has nothing to correspond to it. The interruption of the dialogue points to a lacuna between the end of this leaf (line 71) and the beginning of leaf 123. The gap in the action of the play, however, does not seem very long, and the inference which we should naturally draw, that only one leaf is here lost, is made certain by the fact that on the lower margins in very small roman figures the first two extant leaves are numbered i and iii, the numeration then proceeding iv (next leaf unmarked), vi, vij, viij (next leaf unmarked), x, xj—the rest unmarked.

We may thus be certain that our gathering of twelve leaves was preceded by two other leaves containing the beginning of the text of the play. But as no scribe would begin work by writing on a half quarto sheet, either two or more leaves belonging to the play are wanting before its present beginning, or else the play must have originally been written in a miscellany-book, in which it was preceded by some other piece written on the earlier part of the same gathering. The former hypothesis is not impossible, as the text of the play might have been preceded by the speeches of flag-bearing criers or *vexillatores*, announcing its approaching performance. It is, however, equally possible that both this play and that of *Mind, Will and Understanding* were written in different parts of a miscellany-book belonging to Monk Hyngham, though the fact that his doggrel inscription of ownership is written after each of them inclines one at first to think that they were separate units among his possessions.

As it occurs at the end of this play, the inscription above referred to has been partly erased and partly cut through, the lower part of the leaf being supplied with modern paper. Enough, however, of the inscription remains to make it fairly certain that it reads like that at the end of the next play: O liber si quia cui constas forte queretur Hyngham que monacho dices super omnia consto. This apparently is to be translated (I owe the suggestion to Dr. Warner), "O book, if any one by chance asks to whom do you belong, you are to say I belong to Hyngham, above everything which a monk can own." Who Monk Hyngham was we do not know. He may have belonged to Bury St. Edmunds, whence some of the Macro manuscripts are said to have come. It will be noticed that the round date which Dr. Warner suggests for the manuscript agrees exactly with that which, before consulting him, I had put forward as that of the composition of the play. As it is not good enough to be an author's autograph, it is probably a very early copy.

# More Early English Drama from the Groundling Press

*Anonymous*
## The Life and Death of Jack Straw
The Peasants' Revolt of 1381 is one of the great watershed events in English history. This anonymous sixteenth-century play follows the rebels as they march on London to confront the young Richard II.

*Richard Brome*
## The Weeding of Covent Garden
Brome's "city comedy" features a wild cast of drunken Puritans and swordfighting prostitutes, disguised fathers and scheming sons, in the new and controversial neighborhood of Covent Garden.

*Robert Daborne*
## A Christian Turn'd Turk
The true, though well-embellished, story of seventeenth-century pirate John Ward, later Yusuf Rais, who shocked Jacobean England by converting to Islam in 1608.

For more information on the Groundling Press editions, please visit us at:

**www.groundlingpress.com**

Printed in Great Britain
by Amazon

35786289R00063